Forgiveness keeps us in the light of God and keeps our love door open—Bill Bright taught me this truth for more than fifty years.

From the Foreword by
GARY SMALLEY

BILL BRIGHT'S
"THE JOY OF KNOWING GOD"
SERIES

the JOY of TOTAL FORGIVENESS

DR. BILL BRIGHT

The Bible Teacher's Teacher

COOK COMMUNICATIONS MINISTRIES
Colorado Springs, Colorado • Paris, Ontario
KINGSWAY COMMUNICATIONS LTD
Eastbourne, England

Victor® is an imprint of
Cook Communications Ministries,
Colorado Springs, CO 80918
Cook Communications, Paris, Ontario
Kingsway Communications, Eastbourne, England

THE JOY OF TOTAL FORGIVENESS
© 2005 by Bill Bright

First Printing, 2005
Printed in United States of America
1 2 3 4 5 6 7 8 9 10 Printing/Year 09 08 07 06 05

Cover Design: Brand Navigation, LLC

Library of Congress Cataloging-in-Publication Data

Bright, Bill.
    The joy of total forgiveness : the key to guilt-free living / Bill Bright.
        p. cm. -- (The joy of knowing God series ; bk. 5.)
    ISBN 0-7814-4250-8 (pbk.)
    1. Forgiveness of sin. 2. Christian life. I. Title.
    BT795.B73 2005
    234'.5--dc22

                                        2004026882

Dedication

GLOBAL FOUNDING PARTNERS

The Bright Media Foundation continues the multifaceted ministries of Bill and Vonette Bright for generations yet unborn. God has touched and inspired the Brights through the ministries of writers through the centuries. Likewise, they wish to pass along God's message in Jesus Christ as they have experienced it, seeking to inspire, train, and transform lives, thereby helping to fulfill the Great Commission each year until our Lord returns.

Many generous friends have prayed and sacrificed to support the Bright Media Foundation's culturally relevant, creative works, in print and electronic forms. The following persons specifically have helped to establish the foundation. These special friends will always be known as Global Founding Partners *of the Bright Media Foundation.*

Bill and Christie Heavener and family

Stuart and Debra Sue Irby and family

Edward E. Haddock Jr., Edye Murphy-Haddock, and the Haddock family

Acknowledgments

It was my privilege to share fifty-four years, six months, and twenty days of married life with a man who loved Jesus passionately and served Him faithfully. Six months before his home going, Bill initiated what has become "The Joy of Knowing God" series. It was his desire to pass along to future generations the insights God had given him that they, too, could discover God's magnificence and live out the wonderful plan He has for their lives.

"The Joy of Knowing God" series is a collection of Bill Bright's top ten life-changing messages. Millions of people around the world have already benefited greatly from these spiritual truths and are now living the exciting Christian adventure that God desires for each of us.

On behalf of Bill, I want to thank the following team that helped research, compile, edit, and wordsmith the manuscripts and audio scripts in this series: Jim Bramlett, Rebecca Cotton, Eric Metaxas, Sheryl Moon, Cecil Price, Michael Richardson, Eric Stanford, and Rob Suggs.

I also want to thank Bill's longtime friends and Campus Crusade associates Bailey Marks and Ted Martin, who carefully reviewed the scripts and manuscripts for accuracy.

Bill was deeply grateful to Bob Angelotti and Don Stillman of Allegiant Marketing Group for their encouragement to produce this series and their ingenuity in facilitating distribution to so many.

A special thanks to Cook Communications and its team of dedicated professionals who partnered with Bright Media Foundation in this venture, as well as to Steve Laube, who brought us together.

Last but not least, I want to express my appreciation to Helmut Teichert, who worked faithfully and diligently in overseeing this team that Bill's vision would be realized, and to John Nill, CEO of Bright Media, who has helped me navigate the many challenges along this journey.

As a result of the hard work of so many, and especially our wonderful Lord's promise of His grace, I trust that multitudes worldwide will experience a greater joy by knowing God and His ways more fully.

With a grateful heart,
MRS. BILL BRIGHT (VONETTE)

Contents

Foreword

Forgiveness is one of those life-changing, enriching, and very necessary actions that benefits you more than the person you are forgiving. Forgiveness is at the heart of the three main aspects of God's perfect will for all of us: love Him with our whole heart, love others, and love ourselves.

Forgiveness balances all three aspects of His perfect will. He forgives and loves you daily, you forgive and love others daily, and you forgive and love yourself daily. Forgiveness opens the window of God's light and love into our hearts. If we really want to love ourselves, we have no choice but to learn how to forgive others and ourselves. Forgiveness keeps us in the light of God and keeps our love door open.

Bill Bright taught me this truth for more than fifty years. I remember sitting at his feet at Forest Home Christian Center in Southern California back in the 1950s. He was amazingly focused on reaching people for Christ and teaching them how to live the type of Christ-centered life that would bring them the most satisfying and joyful living. He wanted nonbelievers to notice God's love within those who professed to love God and each other.

Bill Bright clearly saw the two meanings of the word forgiveness: being released or pardoned from our offenses toward God or man, and being untied or released from the power of sin and addiction within us that causes us to sin. Forgiveness not only means being pardoned or sent home free from jail even though we don't deserve it—it also means that we are being healed of what put us in jail in the first place.

Just imagine the children of God pardoning each other daily from offenses and then actively praying and helping one another to form new biblical habits of healing so that we don't keep offending each other. What a world that would be! Bill Bright could see such a world, and I know it is possible through the power of God's Holy Spirit living within us.

—GARY SMALLEY

He has removed our rebellious acts as far away from us as the east is from the west.

PSALM 103:12

THE WORLD IS FULL OF PRODIGALS
YEARNING TO COME HOME.

1

Desiring God's Forgiveness

A young man sits huddled against the wall in a dark, filthy alley. If you were to guess his age, you would overshoot it by a decade; he is little more than a teenager. If you were to guess his background, you would undershoot it by several levels of social class; he comes from a wealthy family, regardless of the trappings of poverty he now wears.

If you were to guess his story, you would shake your head sadly, then nod with sad recognition. For this is another tale of restless youth, the chronicle of a young man who burned too brightly too soon, then flamed out; who squandered every gift he was given. This was just another child estranged from his parents, his friends, and his self-respect.

There was a time when life offered him an extraordinary thrill ride. He cashed in every penny he could claim, setting out for the beckoning enchantment of the big city. He never looked back until later, when the city lost its sparkle. He was in a hurry to find the women, the parties, and the good times.

It was all very intoxicating until the day his wallet ran dry.

That day the parties ended abruptly, the doors closed, the women vanished, and the drudgery began—work as he had never known it, hunger beyond anything he had ever imagined, despair deeper than he knew existed.

And now he sits in the corner of the forsaken alley with layers of dirt beneath his fingernails. He has no clothes but those on his back, the ragged remnant of a once-stylish wardrobe. He has no friends but the animals in whose company he scrambles among the scraps of discarded food. And he has no hope, no hope at all—except for one desperate dream.

Yes, his thoughts have turned homeward at last. He thinks of his family constantly, but he feels a separation far greater than the hundreds of miles between them. How can he expect anything from them, after all? He demanded his share of his father's hard-earned savings—the fruit of a lifetime of work—and used them to sully a once-proud family name. He violated every principle they taught him. He cut himself off from those who loved him the most, those to whom he owed *everything*.

We all stand in the place of that tortured young man.

The thin, starving young man closes his eyes and concentrates on the face of his father, the loving eyes of his mother, and the playful laughter of his brothers and sisters. Tears begin to fall from those darkened sockets. And when he opens his eyes, he discovers he has risen to his feet, emerged from the alley, and set his face on the homeward road. Does he really hope—or is this simply abandonment to the last resort? Is he walking the path to redemption—or pushing himself toward total rejection? If forgiveness, by some miracle, is offered, what dues must be paid? What penance must be suffered?

He nears the family home and is astonished to see his father running out to greet him. There are no harsh words of condemnation awaiting him—only loving arms, a wildly joyful celebration, a delicious feast, a new wardrobe, and a fresh start with a future completely free of guilt or remorse. This young man is on the verge of discovering the incredible power of total forgiveness. And that wonderful journey began for him on the day he *desired* forgiveness enough to come to humbly receive it.

YOUR STORY OF GRACE

Perhaps you have already recognized this beloved old story. The world's greatest storyteller, Jesus Christ, told it some twenty centuries ago. Perhaps more than any other story, the parable of the prodigal son captures the essence of what it means to experience the grace and forgiveness of our almighty Lord and Creator. For we all stand in the place of that tortured young man.

True, you and I may not have traveled to any faraway cities and abandoned ourselves to licentious living. But, like the prodigal, we feel the terrible burden of guilt and the need for forgiveness. We have fallen into sin—which the Bible explains as "missing the mark." We have missed the mark that God expected of us. We have missed the mark that people expected. We have even missed the mark, over and over, that we set for ourselves. So we feel the burning need for forgiveness from all three wronged parties: God, others, and ourselves.

We have yearned to be free of that aching burden. But there have always been those dark moments when we wondered whether such forgiveness is even available. After all, when someone wrongs us in some way, we are not perfect about forgiving, are we? We have held our share of grudges toward those who have dealt with us cruelly. We have struck back in anger more than once. That raises the question: If others are slow to forgive, if we ourselves are slow to forgive, then what about God? And if He will not forgive, where does that leave us in this world and the next one?

Yet the Bible reassures us on this matter. We are told that our sins are forgiven. We are told "He has removed our rebellious acts as far away from us as the east is from the west" (Psalm 103:12). We are told that He chooses to look upon the purity of Christ rather than the sinfulness we wear like the prodigal's shabby clothes. But sometimes it seems too good to be true! Can we be truly, totally, completely, permanently forgiven?

BELIEVE IT!

If only we would believe in total forgiveness! Many of us go on living as if it is not true. It is one thing to grasp the biblical concept intellectually; it is another to let the truth of it permeate our very hearts and souls. If we could do that—if we could stand boldly and freely on the total forgiveness of God— then miracles would happen.

Do you ever find it difficult to really believe that you have *total* forgiveness for your sins in Jesus Christ? You may believe it intellectually and theologically, but what about deep within your heart? Do you behave as if you are totally forgiven, or is there a part of you that is not so sure?

God's Word offers us a perfect example from an experience in the life of our Savior. Imagine yourself in the crowd,

listening to Jesus speak and feeling the power of His personality, when the following commotion breaks out:

> Some men came carrying a paralyzed man on a sleeping
> mat. They tried to push through the crowd to Jesus, but
> they couldn't reach him. So they went up to the roof, took
> off some tiles, and lowered the sick man down into the
> crowd, still on his mat, right in front of Jesus. Seeing their
> faith, Jesus said to the man, "Son, your sins are forgiven."
>
> "Who does this man think he is?" the Pharisees and
> teachers of religious law said to each other. "This is blas-
> phemy! Who but God can forgive sins?"
>
> Jesus knew what they were thinking, so he asked them,
> "Why do you think this is blasphemy? Is it easier to say,
> 'Your sins are forgiven' or 'Get up and walk'? I will prove
> that I, the Son of Man, have the authority on earth to
> forgive sins." Then Jesus turned to the paralyzed man and
> said, "Stand up, take your mat, and go on home, because
> you are healed!"
>
> LUKE 5:18–24

What a marvelous illustration of God's willingness to forgive. We see what happens when total forgiveness is applied:
Radical change occurs. A man who has been paralyzed all his
life rises up and walks. This same power, through the forgiveness of Christ, has already been offered to you. You need only
take hold of it, and you will rise up and walk an entirely new
path.

COME HOME

Perhaps you have heard the story of another prodigal, this one named Henry. Henry, too, had left home in unhappy circumstances. A cash inheritance was not at the center of the issue—just a painful disagreement between his father and him. Cold, harsh words were spoken, primarily by Henry. At one point he nearly struck his father, but his weeping mother came between them.

We will not be disappointed—for there is one Father who waits for us all.

Like so many young people, Henry slammed the front door and left his family with no real plans except the bitter resolve never to speak to his father again. Mother pleaded with him to wait; his brothers and sisters reasoned with him to cool down. But he could not hear them. He could hear only the angry pounding of his own heart and feel the heat of his burning anger.

A year passed, and Henry never returned. His family grieved silently until the father could no longer stand the waiting and the wondering. He was tormented by inner speculation over the fate of his estranged son. So he set out to find him. City by city he journeyed, asking questions and following a cold trail. Finally there was word that his son had settled, after months of wanderings, in a certain town of medium size. Henry's father hunted the streets for days, studying every face that passed him. There were moments when he thought he had spotted his son, but when the figure approached, it was never Henry.

Finally Henry's father took what remained of his meager pocket money and placed a prominent advertisement in the local newspaper. It read, "Henry, all is forgiven. Your father longs to see you and hold you in his arms again. Tomorrow at noon, please come to the top of the hill overlooking the northwestern corner of town, and we will be lovingly reconciled." He signed the note, "Your father." He made multiple copies of the same message and placed them in prominent areas throughout town.

The next day at noon, atop that hill, Henry's son returned. But he was not alone.

Dozens of other young men named Henry had climbed the hill. They were all disappointed, because each one thought it was his father who had offered forgiveness and reconciliation.

The world is full of prodigals yearning to come home, full of Henrys waiting and wondering if forgiveness is somehow available. I praise our wonderful God for the assurance that such grace is freely given to us. This book is written for all the Henrys who stand in need of forgiveness, for I know that you and I are among them. We come to the top of this hill, hoping and praying that we will find the reconciliation for which our hearts yearn. And we will not be disappointed—for there is one Father who waits for us all. There is one Father who set out to rescue us and bring us home to Himself, in the only possible way. Atop another hill, 2,000 years ago, He set a cross in the ground and suffered and died upon it so that we could be forgiven.

FORGIVENESS IS FOREVER

My hope and my prayer are that this book will help you accomplish several crucial things in your life:

- Desire God's forgiveness, as we explore just how wonderful it is.

- Meet God's requirement, as we examine the only possible way to do so.
- Pursue God's heart, as we learn to value the things that He values.
- Experience God's cleansing, as we learn the powerful process of confession.
- Receive God's grace, as we learn to accept and enjoy the forgiveness He offers.
- Abide in God's freedom, as we learn the amazing truth that forgiveness is forever.

2

Receiving God's Forgiveness

Have you ever questioned Christ's forgiveness? If so, I
have good news for you: Christ's death, in your place,
is the basis for your forgiveness. Because of Christ's
substitutionary death on the cross, your forgiveness is not
merely a hope. It is fact! Your moral failures do not enter the
equation at all.

Christ paid the price for all of your sins—totally, once and
for all. If you are a Christian, all of your sins—past, present,
and future—have been forgiven. You cannot add anything to
what Christ has already done for you. Pleadings, tears, personal efforts, and religious ritual cannot reconcile you to God.
Reconciliation has already taken place—the moment you confessed your sins and placed your faith in Christ as your Savior
and Lord.

Hebrews 10 proclaims:

Under this new plan we have been forgiven and made
clean by Christ's dying for us once and for all.... For by
that one offering he made forever perfect in the sight of

God all those whom he is making holy.... Now, when sins
have once been forever forgiven and forgotten, there is no
need to offer more sacrifices to get rid of them.

HEBREWS 10:10, 14, 18 TLB

Before a person sets out on a journey, he or she must take
stock of the starting point. We must know where we are in
order to think about where we are going. In the journey of total
forgiveness, we must begin at the point of personal need—
your own need.

PAID IN FULL

Maybe you are finding it difficult to believe in your heart
that your sin has been paid for. Perhaps you are thinking, "I have lustful thoughts toward another person." Or, "I've
been taking the Lord's name in vain my whole life. God won't
forgive that, will He?"

The fact is, if you have placed your trust in Christ, He has
already forgiven you. You simply need to claim His forgiveness
and believe His promise. And what a promise it is:

> For as high as the heavens are above the earth,
> so great is his love for those who fear him;
> as far as the east is from the west,
> so far has he removed our transgressions from us.

PSALM 103:11–12 NIV

That's the forgiveness God offers. And think of it! It became
yours the moment you believed in Jesus Christ as your Savior
and as an act of your will received Him by faith into your life as
your Lord and Master. Only through Jesus can you experience
God's love and forgiveness. Let me explain why.

Jesus did not live on earth just to prove He is God. He came to give you eternal life, to offer you forgiveness and set you free from sin and guilt, to give you a full and meaningful life here. And it's because Jesus is God that He can provide forgiveness from sin and enable you to live abundantly.

In a conversation with a religious leader of His day, Jesus said, "For God so loved the world that he gave his one and only Son, that whoever believes in him shall not perish but have eternal life. For God did not send his Son into the world to condemn the world, but to save the world through him" (John 3:16–17 NIV).

The apostle Paul wrote, "Therefore, there is now no condemnation for those who are in Christ Jesus, because through Christ Jesus the law of the Spirit of life set me free from the law of sin and death" (Romans 8:1–2 NIV).

FEELINGS

You too can discover the same freedom that Paul found. But you do not do it by feelings. You may feel guilty, but God wants you to have faith in what He has declared in His Holy Word. Faith in His promise of forgiveness to you in Jesus Christ is all that is necessary. Feelings will follow, but faith has to lead.

Likewise, lack of a guilty conscience does not make you innocent. Many people feel no guilt for their sins, so they assume this means they are not guilty and they do not need to be saved from any sins. But they could not be more wrong. Feelings are deceptive. God wants us to have faith in Him and in His Word to us. Our feelings will follow. But whatever your feelings are right now, Scripture is clear that we are sinners and it's clear that through faith in Jesus we are totally forgiven from our sins.

And remember, the only way you can be forgiven is by faith in Jesus. You cannot achieve forgiveness through your own efforts to be good. That will fail every time. The best person in the world cannot hope to get to heaven on his or her own track record. Only faith in Jesus can bridge the gap that our sins have made.

PUT IT TO WORK

Where does your journey begin? Before you continue reading this book, I urge you to spend time in prayer and reflection, asking God to help you attain honest answers to the following questions.

1. Have you experienced the salvation that only Christ can offer? If you are unsure, I urge you to read *The Joy of Finding Jesus* (book two of this "Joy of Knowing God" series).

2. If you are a born-again believer and follower of Christ, reflect on whether you truly know you are forgiven by God. What is your personal image or conception of Him as you pray? What emotions do you have about God? Would you say you feel more loving acceptance by God or more guilty separation? Draw a line with LA at one end (loving acceptance) and GS at the other (guilty separation). Mark the place on the line where you believe your relationship rests.

3. List the five people you interact with most frequently. Evaluate your relationship with each one. What unforgiven acts or attitudes have become obstacles? How forgiving have you been with each person? How well have you accepted their forgiveness (if offered) and moved on?

4. When have you suffered the greatest personal, private guilt? When have you found it most difficult to forgive yourself? How have these mind-sets affected your emotions and your life? What makes it most difficult for you to forgive yourself?

5. Write a covenant prayer—that is, a prayer of contractual promise—to God about the wonderful breakthroughs He wants to make in your life during these next few days. Assure Him that you will be completely open to the changes He wants to make and the love He wants to give you. Ask your precious heavenly Father to help you grasp the awesome, liberating powers of His grace and forgiveness so that your life will be revolutionized and your service to Him will be extraordinary.

Some people talk as if faith in anything is enough—faith in faith itself. Clearly, that does not work. On a winter day, a man can have great faith that the ice on a lake will support his weight. With great faith he can boldly walk out on thin ice and with great faith he can continue walking as the ice cracks. But his faith will only get him miserably cold and wet. You must place your faith, weak or strong, in an object that is worth trusting.

The object of a Christian's faith is the Lord Jesus Christ and His holy, inspired Word. Only He has the power to deliver you from a worldly life to a relationship of great joy and fruitful blessings.

You must place your faith in a trustworthy God and His Word. The better you get to know God, the more you will trust Him. And the more you trust Him, the more you will experience His selfless love and limitless power.

DARKNESS AND LIGHT CANNOT COEXIST

If you were making a journey to the very throne of God, imagine the travel plans you must undertake. Let us begin with the end in mind—the very presence of our loving Father. What is He like? A study of His attributes will leave you trembling with awe and wonder.

That is why Thomas Aquinas, the medieval theologian, literally stopped writing about his Father. Aquinas had been composing the *Summa Theologica*, one of the great milestones of Western civilization. It had already run to thirty-eight treatises and 3,000 articles. He wanted to gather together all the world's truth as it related to the Creator of the universe. He had filled the shelves with volume after volume.

But one day Aquinas stopped writing. While celebrating

Mass in the chapel of Saint Thomas, on December 6, 1273, the Lord gave the scholar a fleeting glimpse of His glory, just as He had given Moses on the mountain thousands of years before. He knew in a flash that his efforts to capture the totality of God in book form were vain and childish. "All my work seems as so much straw," he said.

The greatness of God cannot be fathomed. It cannot be contained by the human mind, nor can we even come close to doing so with our tiny, fragile human minds. To try it—though we reflect on His greatness and praise Him daily—is like attempting to gather the Atlantic Ocean in a teacup. His perfection is absolute. His powers are unlimited. He rules our universe from outside our own confines within time and space, which are merely His creations.

Here is the point: Because He is perfect, the faintest tinge of darkness cannot coexist in His presence. Only light and purity can surround the domain of the throne of God—the destination of our journey. Oh, how He longs to accept us into His arms and His kingdom. But we must attain His standard of purity and perfection; otherwise we can only be destroyed.

FREE INDEED!

And that brings us to our starting point: you. Well, you can already see that the journey is an imposing one. Try this exercise: Take inventory of every little thing in your life that must change before you can walk into that throne room. Take as much time as you need; you will need plenty! You might begin by listing every sin you have ever committed. If you take the proper definition of sin (which we will undertake shortly), you will see that each of us stumbles numerous times every day. You were born in a fallen state, meaning you have a predisposition to sin. To stand in righteousness and per-fection before your Lord and avoid judgment, you would need to account for every one of those blemishes. You would have to free your mind and heart from every stain they have left.

As you can see, the matter is hopeless, no matter who you are and how well you have tried to live. "For all have sinned; all fall short of God's glorious standard" (Romans 3:23). We can never measure up to those standards on our own. We might as well build a stepladder to the moon. The truth is that, left to ourselves, you and I are slaves to sin.

> *Here was a man who, though successful by any worldly standard, had been a slave to multiple cruel masters.*

How can you make the journey to forgiveness and recon-ciliation with God? To help answer that question, allow me to tell you about a friend of mine who discovered the right road.

Shortly after Vonette and I started Campus Crusade for Christ at UCLA, I met a very wealthy man. He owned five newspapers and seemed to have it all, with all the power and possessions a person could want or need. In truth, his life was in chaos. He was an alcoholic and he had already been married and divorced twice. Now his current marriage was on the rocks. My friend felt completely enslaved by sin and failure.

One night, he and his wife accompanied me to a church service. When I gave the invitation to receive Christ, the two of them slipped out the door. I was silent as we walked through the parking lot afterward, but my friend spoke up. He wanted to know if it was too late for him and his wife to receive Christ. You can imagine my answer. We drove home, got down on our knees, and this dear couple invited Christ into their hearts.

From that point on, he began to read his Bible for hours.

He never took another drink of alcohol. And he became one of the most influential businessmen I have ever known. He generously spent a large part of his wealth to promote the Presidential Prayer Breakfast and to sponsor World Vision banquets for needy children. He ministered with me on skid row and in jails. He regularly led other businessmen to Christ. God used him mightily to reach thousands of leading businessmen for Christ and seemed to have some new and thrilling purpose for him every day. My friend was happier and more energetic than he had ever been. Truly, his sins were forgiven and he became a new creature.

It was a total change, but it came only when he reached the point when he desired freedom and forgiveness more than anything else in the world. It came when he was willing to fall on his knees, resign his failed leadership of his own life, and let Christ be Lord forever. Here was a man who, though successful by any worldly standard, had been a slave to multiple cruel masters: alcohol, power, worldly relationships, and his own guilt. But when the Son sets us free, we are free indeed. Every one of us can live as vibrantly and fruitfully as my friend, if we will only live by that same power.

The Cost of Your Salvation

Jesus offers forgiveness to sinners freely, but it is not without great cost to Himself.

On May 21, 1946, in Los Alamos, a young scientist named Louis Slotin diligently prepared for an atomic test. Before this important test could be conducted in the waters of the South Pacific, he needed to determine the critical mass—the amount of U-235—necessary to begin an atomic chain reaction. He had conducted that same experiment several times before.

Each time, he would push the two hemispheres of uranium together. Then, just as the mass became critical, he would push them apart with a screwdriver. But on this day, just as the material became critical, the screwdriver slipped! The two hemispheres of uranium came too close, and the room was filled with a bluish haze.

Without thinking of his own safety, Slotin tore the two hemispheres apart with his bare hands, interrupting the chain reaction. By placing himself in the center of the deadly nuclear reaction, he saved the lives of the seven other people in the room.

As he waited to be taken to the hospital, Slotin calmly told his companion, "You'll come through all right. But I haven't the faintest chance myself." Nine days later he died in agony.

Almost 2,000 years ago, Jesus Christ took upon Himself sin's "critical mass" and endured an agonizing death. By this act, He broke the chain reaction. Christ's sacrifice and triumphant resurrection broke the power of sin in our lives and made us right with God. Because of His sacrifice, our nature has been transformed and our identity has been changed. God no longer sees us as sinners, but as saints.

In a conversation with a religious leader of His day, Jesus said, "God so loved the world that he gave his one and only Son, that whoever believes in him shall not perish but have eternal life. For God did not send his Son into the world to condemn the world, but to save the world through him" (John 3:16–17 NIV). The great bridge has been built. A way was established for you and me to be cleansed from the terrible stain of our sin and to experience the forgiveness we crave.

How could that canyon ever be bridged—the wide canyon between your sin and His holiness?

Jesus said, "the greatest love is shown when people lay down their lives for their friends" (John 15:13). During the Vietnam conflict, the Congressional Medal of Honor was awarded posthumously to a soldier who paid the highest price possible. A live hand grenade landed in a ditch where he and several other soldiers were positioned. There was no time to grab the grenade and hurl it away. So, in order to save his brothers in arms, the courageous infantryman threw himself over the exploding grenade. He died immediately, of course, but he saved many other lives.

Christ made that same kind of sacrifice, but on a global scale. Remember that His life and heart were pure and without sin. He—and only He—could stand pure and stainless at the throne of His Father. Yet He renounced His rightful status and laid down His life, covering the sin—more explosive than any bomb—that would have destroyed each of us:

> This includes you who were once so far away from God.
> You were his enemies, separated from him by your evil
> thoughts and actions, yet now he has brought you back as
> his friends. He has done this through his death on the cross
> in his own human body. As a result, he has brought you
> into the very presence of God, and you are holy and
> blameless as you stand before him without a single fault.
>
> COLOSSIANS 1:21–22

SET APART FOR GOD

Your sinful nature kept you from coming into God's presence. "For the wages of sin is death, but the free gift of God is eternal life through Christ Jesus our Lord" (Romans

6:23). In other words, you have earned total destruction, but you have received total forgiveness—the only kind that could save you. You received it through the total sacrifice of the only One totally qualified. Christ paid the highest price for the fullest forgiveness for the least worthy.

Your Father knew you could not come home. He was like Henry's father. He knew that you had traveled to an evil place and fallen into the slavery of sin. You needed rescuing, so He came to set you free. But sin has consequence. We as His fallen children bore the mark of all our rebellion and failure. It was not as if He could simply disregard all the damage that had been done. Remember, in His holy presence there can be only perfection.

> *God took all of your sins— past, present, and future—and nailed them to Christ's cross.*

God's Holy Word tells us that Jesus Christ, through His death on the cross, has set us free—free from sin, free from the law, free from the bondage of guilt that sin and the law bring.

The Bible explains, "You were dead because of your sins and because your sinful nature was not yet cut away. Then God made you alive with Christ. He forgave all our sins. He canceled the record that contained the charges against us. He took it and destroyed it by nailing it to Christ's cross" (Colossians 2:13–14).

When Christ died on the cross, He did not pay for just the small sins or only some of your sins. God took all of your sins— past, present, and future—and nailed them to Christ's cross.

In God's eyes, that old self of yours is dead indeed. It is as if that sinful version of you never lived. God chooses to see all the perfection and purity of His own beloved Son, and He is willing to make available to you all the endowments of an heir to the kingdom of heaven. How marvelous that all of our sins have been washed away because of the sacrifice of our loving Savior. The Bible proclaims, "Now your sins have been washed away, and you have been set apart for God. You have been made right with God because of what the Lord Jesus Christ and the Spirit of our God have done for you" (1 Corinthians 6:11). Jesus sacrificed His life and covered us with His blood so we could be forgiven of our sins.

COVERED BY THE BLOOD

What exactly does it mean to be "covered with the blood" of Christ? The powerful minister Henry A. Ironside explains it well when he recalls a time he preached in a small town in Washington. While there, he was the guest of friends who raised sheep. It was lambing season. One morning he watched the new lambs play in the meadow. One lamb especially caught his attention. It appeared to have six legs and its fleece hung loosely from its body. When the preacher mentioned this curiosity, one of the herders caught the lamb and brought it to him. Then the mystery was revealed. Draped across the lamb was the fleece of another lamb that had died from a rattlesnake bite. The odd-looking lamb was an orphan, and although the herders had tried to convince the dead lamb's mother to take care of the orphan, the old ewe refused because she did not recognize the lamb's smell. It was not until the herders skinned her own lamb and draped the fleece over the living lamb that she adopted the orphaned lamb as her own.

Jesus sacrificed His life and covered us with His blood so we could be forgiven of our sins. When God looks at us, He sees the righteousness of His perfect, beloved Son. Because of Christ, God is willing to adopt us as His own.

FREEDOM

Not only are we declared free from sin, but we are free from the law. What does that mean? It means we need not live under the crushing burden of trying to please God through perfect behavior. We never can do that, and we never could. But Christ has purified us through His death on the cross, and we are forgiven from all our sins and failures—past, present, and future. Not that we are freed to sin boldly; quite the reverse. We are freed to try to please Him all the more from hearts of overflowing gratitude. We walk in the power and presence of His Holy Spirit, who leads us to live more and more in a way that will please our Father.

"So if the Son sets you free, you will indeed be free" (John 8:36). That means totally free—from sin, from guilt, and from the impossible requirements of the law.

The question is, *Do you desire that forgiveness enough to accept it?*

ALREADY DONE

On June 6, 1944, the Allied Expeditionary Force, composed of armies from various countries, invaded France on the beaches of Normandy. Adolf Hitler's armed forces had spread their reign of terror throughout Europe, and those beaches were heavily guarded. But many thousands of soldiers gave their lives that day to liberate Europe and to bring freedom to its people. Rommel, Hitler's field general, confided to his subordinates that the moment the D-Day invasion succeeded, he knew the war was lost for his side. There would be much more fighting, many more battles, and the Axis forces would even win a few. But the great sacrifice had been made; the blood of Allied soldiers had brought defeat to the reign of fear.

In spiritual terms, Christ provided that same liberation. The difference is that He provided it supernaturally and eternally. When He invaded the world, He broke the hold of the Enemy upon our souls. His blood provided the sacrifice. He liberated us to experience forgiveness, love, and power through the Holy Spirit. The Devil still lives and fights, but the war has been won in our favor.

Our problem comes in not realizing or understanding that

PUT IT TO WORK

I encourage you to spend time reflecting on this chapter. Let its truth fill you so that you never forget: You will remain imperfect, but in the heavenly realms God sees you as pure and unblemished, like His Son. Unless you grasp this truth with all its implications, you will never know the radical power of total forgiveness.

When you realize how God regards you, you hold in your hand the key to knowing and loving yourself in a whole new way. Can you imagine how different your life would be if you saw yourself as God sees you? The following exercises will help you begin to internalize the amazing truth of your new standing before God.

1. Begin by listing all the attributes of God you can imagine. Stop to offer thanksgiving and praise that we can know such a wonderful Father. Reflect on the majesty and purity of His presence, and spend time worshiping Him. You should begin every spiritual exercise this way, for we must know and acknowledge who God is before we can come to any new truth about ourselves.

2. Make a list of your sins. But rather than the impossible goal of being complete, list ten of the major ones that concern you the most. These can be attitudes, habits, or anything in your life that you know dishonors God in any way. Spend time praying to God about each one, confessing them honestly before Him.

state of affairs. We continue to struggle as if Christ had not won the victory. We continue to stand accused as if the Devil held any power over us whatsoever—which, my friends, he does not. The only hope for our rescue came through the invasion of this dark world by Christ, and we must depend on Him and only Him.

The apostle Paul wrote, "There is now no condemnation for those who are in Christ Jesus, because through Christ Jesus the law of the Spirit of life set me free from the law of sin and death" (Romans 8:1–2 NIV).

3. Go over each item on that list and concentrate on Christ's blood shed to forgive you for that sin. Use a red pen and make a line through each one as you affirm that God will no longer see that sin, you are forgiven for it, and you will "go and sin no more" (John 8:11). Spend as much time as you need to fully embrace God's forgiveness. Gifts are given, but they must also be consciously accepted. Spend more time thanking God for His grace and provision.

4. Think about the next few days and weeks: family life, work, school, or any circles in which you find yourself. Realize that any sin you commit is already forgiven by virtue of Christ's sacrifice. Write down mistakes you could possibly make, poor attitudes you could possibly have, or any transgression you might commit. Acknowledge God's forgiveness and ask for His power in living in His victory.

5. Imagine yourself standing in the presence of God, joyfully and without shame, knowing that your Father regards you as He does His own Son. Offer a prayer like this one, in your own words: *Most precious and loving Father, I realize that I am totally forgiven. I realize that You have removed my sins as far as the east is from the west. I can see myself as You see me—purely and without sin—and I choose to live the rest of this day in the light of that fact. I make a covenant right now to rise each morning, spend time with You, and live as a holy, chosen child of the King rather than a fallen, confused soul of this world. In Your strength and guidance, I shall do so. Amen.*

THE ONLY WAY

D o you see the qualifying terms of those verses? *Whoever believes in him; those who are in Christ Jesus.* Total forgiveness comes totally from Christ and is totally unavailable elsewhere. This means there is one bridge, and only one bridge, to cross that spiritual canyon that separates us from God and forgiveness. We must let the cross span the gap and accept the way that Christ has offered.

It is quite important to understand what changes occur when we make that acceptance. Do we become perfect? No, not at all. We will remain human, and we will still stumble, though we should never again be slaves to sin. Are God's standards any less perfect? No, not at all. The difference is that God looks at us and sees the purity of Christ because He looked at His Son's cross and allowed the punishment of all our sins.

3

Pursuing God's Heart

Many people today deny the stain of sin in their lives. Others attempt to ignore sin's smudge by saying, "It's not so bad." Some try to excuse their blemish claiming, "I'm no worse than anyone else." And many others attempt their own methods to overcome sin's blot in their lives. But the only hope anyone has to overcome sin is a supernatural cleansing—the cleansing that only God can perform through His Son, the Lord Jesus, who died and shed His blood for our sins.

Consider King David: He lived about 3,000 years ago, but to this day we remember him as a "man after God's own heart." He was a gifted man, a natural and eloquent communicator, a born athlete, a military hero, and a devotee of fine art and music. Only once in several generations will such a gifted, natural-born leader emerge to lead his country to greatness.

And that is exactly what he did. Under his able guidance, this nation took its place among the prosperous empires of the world. Its army was feared. Its wealth was impressive. The leader established a regime that seemed capable of holding power for many decades. No wonder the people loved him so! He was one of the giants of his time, the most honored and accomplished of the world's leaders.

Yet behind the scenes, things were different. This is a man who committed adultery and murder, then attempted to bury his actions in a web of lies. Surely his transgressions leaked out to the public. Even if the government succeeded in white-washing his actions through a careful cover-up, God would know. Our righteous Lord judges the sins of men's hearts. We expect Him to cast down this fraud of a leader. So what did God say about the man?

He called the leader "a man after my own heart" (Acts 13:22). He loved this leader, King David, in a special way. He allowed him to stay in power and continued to work through him.

How can this be? David committed premeditated, pre-planned adultery with a beautiful married woman named Bathsheba. Then, when the woman became pregnant, David got involved in a web of dishonest machinations to cover up his sin and make it appear that the woman's husband, Uriah, was the child's true father. When these efforts failed, David simply planned out a hasty death for Uriah. He did so by placing the man, a loyal soldier who revered David, on the front lines of battle. Thus, in one terrible tangle of actions and reactions, David broke three of the Ten Commandments.

REPENTANCE

How can it be that a man who did such awful things was ever described so lovingly in Scripture as a man after God's own heart?

We would rightfully demand accountability of any leader (or any human being, for that matter) who was caught in such flagrant sin. Did God allow these sins to go unpunished? Did He somehow play favorites and hold David to a lower standard of righteousness?

No, He did not. For one thing, David's sin cost him his unborn child. There was a terrible price paid for the king's transgressions. But David avoided a more sweeping judgment because of something that happened in his heart: He repented. Sorrowful repentance paved the way for total forgiveness. David saw the horror of his sin—he admitted it—and he was truly repentant.

After Nathan the prophet confronted the king with his wickedness, the full burden of his awful guilt overwhelmed David. Psalm 51 carries the powerful testimony of his remorse, for it holds the words of the prayer he offered before God in the wake of facing a terrible conscience:

> Have mercy on me, O God,
> because of your unfailing love.
> Because of your great compassion,
> blot out the stain of my sins.
> Wash me clean from my guilt.
> Purify me from my sin.
> For I recognize my shameful deeds—
> they haunt me day and night.
> Against you, and you alone, have I sinned;
> I have done what is evil in your sight.
> You will be proved right in what you say,
> and your judgment against me is just.
>
> PSALM 51:1–4

And in Psalm 32 he expresses the joy he felt over God's love and forgiveness:

> What happiness for those whose guilt has been forgiven! What joys when sins are covered over! What relief for those who have confessed their sins and God has cleared their record.
>
> There was a time when I wouldn't admit what a sinner I was. But my dishonesty made me miserable and filled my days with frustration. All day and all night your hand was heavy on me. My strength evaporated like water on a sunny day until I finally admitted all my sins to you and stopped trying to hide them. I said to myself, "I will confess them to the Lord." And you forgave me! All my guilt is gone.
>
> PSALM 32:1–5 TLB

CHANGE OF HEART

David, from the depths of his experience, shares this admonition from his heart: "Now I say that each believer should confess his sins to God when he is aware of them, while there is time to be forgiven. Judgment will not touch him if he does" (Psalm 32:6 TLB). I am concerned about multitudes of Christians whose hearts do not change when they are being disciplined by God for unconfessed sins. They may be experiencing all sorts of things as a result of their sins: It might be financial reverses, physical illnesses, or any other kinds of trouble—all because they are being disobedient to Him, and He is trying to get their attention so that He can bless and enrich their lives.

We stand before God in purity and righteousness, regardless of the sins we have committed. When Christ set us free, we became truly free. The Lord refuses to look upon our sins as long as we allow them to be covered by the blood of Christ.

We as Christians celebrate this wonderful truth, but stumbling blocks immediately follow. Inevitably we sin again, whether in some small way or in something of the magnitude of David's awful transgression. We quickly forget that *all* our sins, including the future ones, are covered. And therefore we are burdened anew by guilt and remorse. We imagine the wrath of God, and we allow our failure to become an obstacle in our relationship to Him. Quite often, this fresh evidence of sin discourages people until they drift away from God. More and more they pray less and less. They avoid church and God's Word. All these things remind them of their guilty conscience.

But how much will God forgive? All the sin we might commit. How deep will that forgiveness go? To the depth of the worst transgressions we could imagine. We cannot "over-sin" His forgiveness.

THE DAVID PRINCIPLE

This is not to say that our sins have no consequences in this world. They most certainly do. And God disciplines us when we need it. It is not that He is *unaware* of our transgressions, simply that He refuses to *regard* them in judgment. We need a clear understanding of how God handles ongoing sin and how we should handle it.

I encourage you to do what I do when I experience difficulties—turn to the Lord and ask, "Lord, is there sin in my life that is making it necessary for You to discipline me?" The Scriptures say that God disciplines those whom He loves (Hebrews 12:6). When you stumble in some way, it is important to look into the mirror of God's Word and to confess any sin that He reveals. This is when the "David Principle"—repentance, confession, and forgiveness—can make all the difference in your life. Knowing these scriptural strategies will keep you closer to God. As a matter of fact, not only will you avoid drifting away from Him, but He will use your failure and repentance to make you stronger and wiser than ever. In other words, your failures need not be stumbling blocks of faith; instead, they can be stepping-stones to genuine spiritual growth.

> *He will use your failure and repentance to make you stronger and wiser than ever.*

Imagine that you come home from a long day of work. You are tired and not at your best. Your spouse makes some remark that causes you to snap back an unfriendly reply, words that you realize are inappropriate. Immediately you feel that gentle tugging at your heart that means the Holy Spirit is showing you your sin. He never accuses; only the Devil does that. He gently, lovingly points to what you have done wrong, and you realize that a child of God can and must behave better, that confession is in order and amends must be made.

In this situation, in the light of your conviction, you call a time-out from whatever you are doing and take a moment to confront your own sin. Simply acknowledge that sin is what it is—forget the excuses. *Sin is sin.*

Then, by faith, simply cast your soul upon Christ. That means affirming that any sin is a sin for which He has died. It is forgiven; the stain has already been scrubbed away. Confess your sin to God, then repent. That means personally turning in the opposite direction and resolving to avoid that sin in the future. Go and apologize to your spouse, and let the Lord teach you a helpful lesson through the whole situation.

"WHY CONFESS IF I'M FORGIVEN?"

God's cleansing from the sins that hinder you opens the way to the abundant, fulfilling life to which Jesus has called you. By faith you can simply claim as true what Jesus Christ has said and done for you. By faith you can view yourself as God views you, as His child—loved, forgiven, and cleansed. By faith you can confess your sins and repent, and by faith you can accept God's forgiveness and cleansing.

Many people become bewildered at this very point. They ask a good question: If Christ has already paid the penalty for my sins, why should I confess them? If they are already fully covered by the atoning blood of Christ—as they are indeed— why take the time to dredge them up and confess them, to regard them in any way when God does not?

Regardless of the misunderstanding of many believers, confession does not bring about forgiveness. Christ has already granted forgiveness for us 2,000 years ago at Calvary. New sin will not remove us from the salvation that God has granted, but it can and will become an obstacle that is destructive to our relationship with our Father. By confessing, we deal with the effect of our sin upon the "here and now." In the heavenly realm, we still stand spotless and pure

If Christ has already paid the penalty for my sins, why should I confess them?

before our Father. But on earth, in the flesh, we do not feel so well! We know our sin has damaged our fellowship with God, with others, and with ourselves. We need a way of facing it and dealing with its real-world effects on us.

By confessing your sin, you act on your faith in God and His Word. Confession does not give you more forgiveness. Christ has already forgiven you once and for all. But by admitting your sins, you establish in your experience what God has done for you through the death of His Son. In other words, the cross gains us our forgiveness; confession claims the power of that forgiveness to help us live a holy and righteous life.

KEEPING CLEAN

Perhaps you spend a great deal of time maintaining a beautiful home. You spend years studying interior decoration, replacing your old furniture with fine antiques, and getting the walls, floors, and even the ceilings as beautiful and perfect as can be. Finally, a magazine sends a photographer out to create a photographic profile of your lovely home. Cable television's HGTV, the network specializing in beautiful homes, films a TV show about your house. And finally you win the prize: Most Beautiful Home of the Year.

As you are centering the attractively framed proclamation on your living room wall, your son walks by, bumps into you, and spills a chocolate milk shake on your spotless carpet. What do you do? Perhaps you smile and say, "Why worry about that mess? It will not cost us the Home of the Year award." Then you turn and leave the room.

Highly unlikely! At this point, it surely means something to you to have a clean home. That chocolate milk shake ruins the whole effect. You will immediately want to scrub it away, though any new stain is irrelevant to the honor you have received.

That is precisely how we feel about sin and confession. Forgiveness has been attained. The war has been won, but we will want to win the battles all the more. Christ has died for us, and we want our lives to be as clean and pure as they can be. Just as homes can slide slowly into untidy disarray, lives can slip more and more away from the close fellowship with the Lord that we need.

ACCOUNTABILITY

John Wesley was one of our most powerful Christian leaders. Under his guidance, Christian believers met together in little communities to keep one another on the right road in life. They challenged each other at the point of their decisions and their spiritual growth. Wesley called this "watching over one another in love." There was nothing harsh or legalistic about it, but believers were determined to hold each other accountable to a life of holiness.

Before a new believer even entered that community of faith, the newcomer would be closely questioned on his or her willingness to be confronted with sins. These believers understood that it is unpleasant to face the ugly sides of our nature, but it is far more unpleasant and damaging to face the results should they go unchecked.

LOVED BY GOD

When Jesus had His last conversation with His assembled disciples in the Upper Room, He prayed this prayer for them: "I have given them the glory you gave me, so that they may be one, as we are—I in them and you in me, all being perfected into one. Then the world will know that you sent me and will understand that you love them as much as you love me" (John 17:22–23).

Think of it! God loves you as much as He loves His only begotten Son, the Lord Jesus Christ. That is a remarkable truth with implications that are staggering. David sinned powerfully, but God's love held even more power. My friend, there is nothing you can do that will remove you from the blanket of total forgiveness that Christ has established for you. And when you stumble and fall, God has provided a way for you to rise to your feet again through confession.

PUT IT TO WORK

Begin living out these truths today by doing the following:

1. Be certain you hold on to your "first love" of Jesus Christ (Revelation 2:4). Think back to the day you first accepted Him into your heart as Lord and Savior. Do you still feel the same love and devotion? If not, work immediately to rekindle the sparks by spending more time with Him. Before you are motivated to pursue the heart of God, you will need to do some maintenance work on your own heart. Spend time reviewing the things God has done in your life. Thank Him and offer Him your praise and worship. Ask Him to renew within you a sense of His presence and His power.

2. Identify the one chronic behavior in your life that you feel serves as the greatest obstacle in your relationship with God. Why is this behavior persistent? Will you trust God to give you victory over it? Claim His power and create a plan for keeping it out of your life, as well as confessing it on the possibility that it does occur.

3. Draw a map of your soul as if it were a household. Since your body is a temple for the Holy Spirit (1 Corinthians 6:19), this is a reasonable analogy. What items in the "household" glorify God the most? Which ones glorify Him the least? What can be done to make this setting a fitting home for God's Spirit? Write down several action steps you can take to make the domain of your life more glorifying to God; then spend

---

We saw in the parable of the prodigal son that God loves you not *when, if,* or *because* you deserve it, but even when you are disobedient and rebellious.

Can it be true? It is true. God's Word cannot lie. When you confess your sins, God, in His unconditional love, welcomes you back and eagerly forgives you. Instead of running away from Him in fear, you can run to His loving arms, confident that He forgives you. No matter what you might have done, if you are honest with God, God can think of you, too, like David, as a person "after his own heart."

David concludes his reflection on confession by attesting, "you are my hiding place; you protect me from trouble. You

time in prayer asking Him to guide you toward holiness through the work of the Holy Spirit.

4. Think about a friend you might choose as an accountability partner. While parents or spouses should always be accountability partners, try to look also to one important person from outside the circle of your family. As John Wesley described it, you need someone to "watch over you in love." Make a resolution to be honest and to trust your friend to hold you accountable for a lifestyle that glorifies God in every way possible. You will also grow spiritually by returning the favor for your partner. Make this a regular meeting of high priority, at least weekly if possible.

5. Spend the next few days praying and reflecting on a new resolution to pursue the heart of God with fresh energy and commitment. Use a prayer like this one: *Lord, more than ever I want Your heart to be my heart. I want to care about the issues and goals that You care about. I want to be a holy temple for Your Spirit in every way and to glorify You with every step I take and every word I speak. I will confess my sins before my fellow believers and before You. I will repent from any sin that comes into my life; and with each week that goes by I will be wiser, stronger, and bolder in proclaiming Your blessed name in this world. Amen.*

surround me with songs of victory" (Psalm 32:7). Through confession and repentance, your life can be that kind of safe and joyful sanctuary.

So, as the writer of Hebrews puts it, "let us strip off every weight that slows us down, especially the sin that so easily hinders our progress. And let us run with endurance the race that God has set before us" (Hebrews 12:1).

4

Experiencing God's Cleansing

In Victor Hugo's classic novel *Les Misérables* is an unforgettable character named Jean Valjean, a man who has attempted to leave a dark, criminal past behind him. Traveling to a new town, Valjean has started over again, built a reputation of respectability, and eventually becomes the mayor. His past is behind him—or is it?

One day news from a neighboring town reaches Jean Valjean. An old man, a thief of apples, has been arrested and misidentified as the notorious fugitive Jean Valjean. Based on that tragic blunder, the old man will be sent to the gallows for execution.

The real Jean Valjean is struck by a true crisis of the soul. He can keep quiet and continue to serve his town faithfully as mayor, thus allowing a relatively innocent man to be punished in his place. Or he can choose to renounce his new life, declare his true identity, and be hanged. As Valjean thinks of it, he can remain in paradise and become a demon, or he can go to hell and become an angel.

In the end, Jean Valjean does the right thing. Just before

the old man is executed, the mayor steps forward and says, "I am Jean Valjean." People in the crowd think he is mad. He looks out upon them and says, "All of you consider me worthy of pity, do you not? When I think what I was on the point of doing, I consider that I am to be envied. God, who is on high, looks down on what I am doing at this moment, and that suffices."

STOPPING SIN IN ITS TRACKS

My friend, it is true that confession is good for the soul—more true than we can ever realize. Like Jean Valjean, we watch as another is accused of the sins we committed. We stand in the crowd and watch Christ crucified, for He has chosen, of His own volition, to pay for all our wrongdoing. He has chosen to let us establish a fresh new life. But what about now? Will we continue to sin? Every time we do so, we crucify Christ anew. Knowing we can live in the power of the Holy Spirit, we choose to disobey God and drive one more nail into the nail-scarred hand.

I cannot bear to do that. Though I can never eliminate sin entirely in this life, I can do two things: I can resolve to live the purest and holiest life possible, and I can confess every sin that does occur in my life. I will know that God, who is on high, looks down upon me and approves. And that will suffice.

This is why I have advocated a process for confession known as "Spiritual Breathing." I believe that sin is urgent. There is no such thing as an inconsequential one, for any sin, no matter how small, drives us further away from our Lord and the only source of true spiritual life. Therefore we cannot afford to push any act of spiritual disobedience to the back shelf for later reference, where it might develop a tighter grip upon the soul. The best way to deal with sin is head on, in person, immediately. The psalmist writes, "If I regard iniquity in my heart, the Lord will not hear" (Psalm 66:18 NKJV).

In the next chapter I will attempt to explain the best strategy I know for cutting off sin in its tracks.

—————— ❖ ——————

IF WE CONFESS OUR SINS, HE IS FAITHFUL
AND JUST AND WILL FORGIVE US OUR SINS AND
PURIFY US FROM ALL UNRIGHTEOUSNESS.

1 JOHN 1:9 NIV

——————————————

5

Spiritual Breathing

One day I was speaking to a friend on a cellular phone. At one point in our conversation, all I could hear was loud static. Some obstruction had interrupted the radio signal, and I missed a portion of what my friend had said. After the car had cleared the obstacle, I could once again hear his voice clearly, and we were able to continue our conversation.

Sin obstructs your communication and relationship with God. When you tolerate sin in your life, you cannot hear God. You become discouraged and confused. Soon you may find yourself operating on your memories of God instead of living in vital interaction with Him. All you need to do to experience God's forgiveness is to confess your sins—"exhale" spiritually. That cleansing breath restores your fellowship with Him.

If you refuse to deal honestly with God by ignoring your sins, you become worldly and are living in the shadows instead of walking in God's light. As 1 John 1:6–7 (TLB) states:

So if we say we are his friends but go on living in spiritual darkness and sin, we are lying. But if we are living in the light of God's presence, just as Christ does, then we have wonderful fellowship and joy with each other, and the blood of Jesus his Son cleanses us from every sin.

SLIPPERY SLOPE

Perhaps you are aware of sins that you have not confessed to God. As a result, you have left your first love for Him. You may feel resentment toward someone. Your relationship with Christ may seem mechanical and routine. Your prayers do not seem to reach God. You read the Bible, but you do not remember what you have read. You may even attempt to witness for Christ, but no one responds.

Our adversary the Devil wants you to avoid taking "little" sins seriously. He wants you to think about it later—always later. He wants you to put together a whole collection of unconfessed sins until they begin to gather momentum, without your realizing it. Like tiny rolling pebbles, these sins gather more debris as they roll down the slope of your life. Neglect prayer today; tell that lie tomorrow; gossip the next day. If you don't bring that problem before God, you will discover that a slippery slope leads to an avalanche in regard to your spiritual condition. One day you will wake up and realize your Lord has become a stranger to you.

KEEP SHORT ACCOUNTS

You cannot totally avoid sin (though, of course, you should live the purest and most righteous life possible), but you can confess your sins immediately and experience forgiveness and restoration before damage is done. To experience God's forgiveness, simply confess your sin and accept His forgiveness by faith. I call this "Spiritual Breathing." Why does it have such a name? We know that breathing is one of the essentials of life. You cannot live for more than a moment if you fail to breathe physically, exhaling carbon dioxide and inhaling fresh air. It is just as essential in the spiritual realm to "exhale" (confess) what is impure and to "inhale" (accept forgiveness) the purity of God's cleansing and restoration. Just as you exhale and inhale physically, so you must also breathe spiritually.

Imagine you have displeased God in some way during your workday. Perhaps you spoke words that were unkind or you failed in some matter of personal responsibility. The Holy Spirit will quickly make you aware of your transgression. At that point, do not wait until a later time to consider the matter. Instead, stop where you are and confess your sin to God. Even if you are driving a car, you can silently acknowledge your wrongdoing to God.

As you offer your misdeed to God, think of it as exhaling spiritually—out with the bad air. Be certain you have truly let it all out, dismissing this sin from your life. As you exhale, recognize it is past and gone and that the Lord will not hold it against you. Then "inhale" the wonderful grace and forgiveness of God, who makes you clean again.

OUT WITH THE BAD AIR

You exhale spiritually when you confess your sins. The Bible promises that if you confess your sins to Him, He is faithful and just to forgive you and to purify you from all unrighteousness (1 John 1:9). Unconfessed sin short-circuits the flow of God's power in your life. Let me illustrate. One day, years ago, as I was operating the controls of my son's electric train, it suddenly stopped running. I could not figure out what was wrong. I took the train apart and put it back together. I pushed the plug in and out of the socket. Nothing happened. Then I discovered that a little piece of metal—a "No Left Turn" sign—had fallen across the tracks, short-circuiting all the electrical power.

To maintain a victorious Christian life, you must keep short accounts with God. By that I mean you confess any sin that enters your life the moment God's Holy Spirit reveals it to you. If you snap at someone in conversation, the Spirit will point it out. Confess it immediately to God, repent, and apologize to your friend. You will be truly amazed by the incredible differences you will immediately see in your life. If you refuse to confess your sin, you become carnal and walk in the shadow instead of in the light of God's love and forgiveness.

To confess your sins means to agree with God about how you have disobeyed Him. Your agreement is threefold.

First, *you agree that your sins are wrong and that they grieve God.* God is holy and will have nothing to do with sin. Although He loves you even though you may have unconfessed sin in your life, you must consider your sin as seriously as He does. Proverbs 14:9 (NIV) says, "Fools mock at making amends for sin." The apostle John writes:

> If we claim to be without sin, we deceive ourselves and the truth is not in us ... If we claim we have not sinned, we make him out to be a liar and his word has no place in our lives.
>
> 1 JOHN 1:8, 10 NIV

Second, *you recognize that God has already forgiven your*

sins through Christ's death and the shedding of His blood on the cross. Confession, then, is an expression of faith and an act of obedience, which results in God making real in your experience what He has already done for you through the death of His Son. This real and ongoing experience of God's forgiveness helps you remain an open channel through which God's love and power can flow.

Third, *you repent.* You change your attitude, which results in a change of action. Through the strength of the Holy Spirit, you turn from your sins and change your conduct. Instead of giving in to the compulsion of your worldly, fleshly nature, you now do what God wants in the power of the Holy Spirit.

In with the Good Air

You change from a worldly Christian to a spiritual Christian by inhaling, appropriating the fullness and power of the Holy Spirit by faith.

How do we truly inhale? As we have seen, forgiveness has already been granted at the cross as a matter between the Father and the Son. When we know that the sin is gone, the Spirit is already helping us to make adjustments so that we will not fall into this trap again, and we feel so wonderfully clean. There are no obstacles between God and us.

If It's Been Awhile …

A friend of mine lives in the Deep South, where the kudzu vine is a common sight along highways. This vine was transplanted from China and quickly spread all across the region. Gardeners know that it takes hard work to keep that kudzu from overrunning a backyard and covering every tree, eventually choking it out. They say that the first year the vine sleeps, the second year it creeps, and the third year it leaps! Think of sin in the same way. It may be as common as the kudzu vine, and it may even look as harmless at the time—but it cannot be allowed to make itself comfortable in the holy temple of your soul. Soon it will slowly creep, and finally it will have you under its power.

Confession is like a good pair of shears. You stand daily as an alert gardener, watching over the garden of your soul. The sharp shears of confession allow you to trim back that deadly vine the moment it breaks the surface, and your garden remains beautiful and pleasing to God, your friends, and yourself.

It's possible that over a period of time you have allowed a series of unconfessed sins to accumulate in your soul. Like that creeping kudzu vine, it strangles you spiritually and cuts you off from intimacy with God. Here is a variation on Spiritual Breathing that has helped thousands of people experience God's love and forgiveness after a prolonged "absence" from Him.

STEP ONE: LIST YOUR SINS

Start by asking the Holy Spirit to reveal to you every sin in your life. Take a pencil and paper and list every sin He brings to mind. As you write, confess sin to God. Tell God about what you did wrong. Whether it was gossiping about a coworker or an adulterous relationship, *tell God!* Tell Him *everything!*

As an example, let's say you wrote down that you remembered one day last week when you had a bad attitude toward a colleague. Then you talked badly about him to others. Write that down. Then just say, "Dear Lord, I admit that I had a bad attitude toward Tony. I was wrong. And I told Donna what a bad person he was. That was wrong too. I'm sorry. Thank You for dying on the cross to forgive my sin."

It is that simple. God is not looking for eloquent words. He's looking for an honest heart. Humble yourself before God as you do this. Give Him time to reveal everything in your life that is displeasing to Him. This list is just between you and God, so be completely honest. Tell Him everything that is wrong.

Your list may include things like this:

- Leaving your first love for God
- Spending little or no time praying or reading and studying God's Word
- Seldom, if ever, witnessing for Christ
- Lacking faith in God
- Having a jealous attitude
- Lusting after material things
- Dealing with others in a spirit of pride
- Acting selfishly
- Being dishonest, lying
- Talking about others behind their backs
- Entertaining immoral thoughts
- Committing sexual sins

Whatever your sin, write it down. And remember, a loving God forgives you—He gave His Son, the Lord Jesus, to die for your sins.

After hearing this message, a young man said, "I didn't believe I needed to make a list. I couldn't think of anything seriously wrong in my life. But when I saw others making their lists, the Spirit of God told me to do the same."

There were no major areas of disobedience in his life, but

he admitted that a lot of little things had dulled the cutting edge of his love and witness for Christ.

He said, "If I hadn't made my list, I would've missed a special blessing from God."

STEP TWO: WRITE 1 JOHN 1:9

After you have written down the sins God reveals, write God's promise of forgiveness from 1 John 1:9 across the list. God promises, "If we confess our sins, he is faithful and just and will forgive us our sins and purify us from all unrighteousness" (NIV).

STEP THREE: ACCEPT HIS FORGIVENESS

When you have completed your time of prayer and confession, accept His forgiveness. Do it by faith. As an illustration of God's forgiveness, destroy the list. Tear it into pieces or burn it to show how completely God has forgiven you.

STEP FOUR: MAKE RESTITUTION

Ask God if you need to make restitution. You may need to apologize for having that bad attitude toward your colleague. You may need to ask someone to forgive you for the way you have treated him or her. You may need to return something you have stolen.

Whatever it is, it is important for you to make restitution to others. You cannot maintain a clear conscience before God if you still have a guilty conscience before people. Confession often includes making restitution.

Here's an example of how this simple process worked in the life of one person.

At the end of a Christian medical meeting on forgiveness, a doctor accepted this challenge. He made his list, wrote out

1 John 1:9, then destroyed the list to symbolize God's complete forgiveness. He was very excited the next morning.

He said, "Last night about midnight a doctor friend of mine came to my room. He told me he'd hated me for years. All the while, he was pretending to be my friend. As he was making his list, God told him that he should come and tell me and ask me to forgive him. So he did. Then we had the most wonderful time of prayer, and God met us in a special way."

IF YOU ARE STILL BURDENED BY GUILT ...

Are you still weighed down by heavy burdens of guilt? Do you sometimes wonder if you will ever experience the love and forgiveness of God that other Christians joyfully profess? If, after you have fully confessed all of your known sins to God, you still feel a sense of guilt, it may be because you have not been completely honest with Him by making a full disclosure. So be sure you are honest with God, and ask Him to reveal anything else that may not have already occurred to you.

As one who has been forgiven, you are righteous before God in Jesus Christ.

Or perhaps you are holding on to false guilt. Perhaps you feel like the man who was stumbling along the road with a heavy pack on his back. Soon, a wagon stopped, and the driver offered to give him a ride. The weary traveler gratefully accepted. But when he climbed onto the wagon, he continued to strain under his heavy load.

"Why don't you take off your pack and rest?" the driver asked.

The discouraged traveler replied, "Oh, I couldn't do that! It would be too much to ask you to carry my load as well as me."

"How foolish," you say. We would not think of responding like that to such an offer, would we? Yet many Christians continue to carry heavy burdens of guilt even after they have entrusted their lives to the Lord Jesus and received His forgiveness.

Frequently we experience hostility or punishment from our family or friends when we fall short of their expectations. If you have truly wronged another person, confessing it and making restitution when necessary will release the guilt. But feelings of guilt will linger if you do not forgive yourself or if you try to live up to the unrealistic expectations of others.

None of us is perfect. But as Christians we do not live in condemnation. As one who has been forgiven, you are righteous before God in Jesus Christ. He wants you to know that and to live as though you know it; He wants you to be free.

6

Forgiven Once and for All

While discussing Spiritual Breathing, I have emphasized the "exhalation" portion: breathing out the "bad air." Let us not forget the good news concerning "inhalation." Have you ever stepped out into the world during a beautiful April day and taken a deep, refreshing breath of springtime air? As wonderful an experience as that is, it cannot compare to the refreshment of God's purification of your soul every time you bring your sin to Him.

On those occasions you can be certain that He is more than pleased with you. His Spirit will let you know what it means to feel truly clean and free as the stain of sin is removed. I cannot imagine living a single day without relying on the process of immediate confession to keep me close to my loving Savior. This strategy alone has paved the way for more spiritual growth and maturity in my life than any other I can name.

LET IT GO

You can know that when you have completed this simple process, any feelings of guilt that remain are not from

God. They are from your enemy Satan. Scripture declares that your sins have been removed as far as the east is from the west (Psalm 103:12). They are buried in the deepest sea (Micah 7:19). God has put them behind His back and remembers them against you no more (Hebrews 8:12; 10:17). Believe it!

There was a young boy who had a pet bird, and one day the bird died. The boy was brokenhearted, and his father and mother decided that instead of allowing their son to be downcast, they would make something memorable of the occasion.

They said, "Let's have a funeral." Calling all the neighborhood children together, they dug a little hole in the ground, put the bird in a box, and buried it with a ceremony. Instead of being downcast, the boy was excited.

But the next day, he went out and dug up the bird to see

ABUNDANT LIFE

Now you are free to experience the abundant life that He promised. Now you can encourage and serve your brothers and sisters in Christ. And now you can enter the harvest fields to enjoy bringing other people to the Lord Jesus, who has done so much for you. That's His will for you. Walk in it with joy.

As you incorporate Spiritual Breathing into your own life, take these steps:

1. Commit the following verse to memory so that you may use it every day. "Search me, O God, and know my heart; test me and know my thoughts. Point out anything in me that offends you, and lead me along the path of everlasting life" (Psalm 139:23–24). Repeating those powerful, divinely inspired words of Scripture will add to your determination to seek God in dealing with daily sin. Incorporate the verse into your daily time with God and use it as often as you need as you go about your day.

2. As you work to make Spiritual Breathing a habit, create personal reminders in your daily life so that you will remember to check your life for unconfessed sin regularly. You might do something as simple as

how it was getting along. His father, however, insisted that he
bury it. So he did. A few days later, the boy went out and dug
up the bird again. This happened several times, and each time
the father would reprimand him. Finally, the father became
angry and said, "Now look, you leave that bird in the ground,
and don't ever dig it up again!"

Are you confessing the same sins over and over again—out
of a sense of guilt—like the little boy digging up that old dead
bird?

God has forgiven all of your sins on the basis of Christ's
death on the cross and the shedding of His blood for your sins.
Whenever Satan accuses you of some act in your past that has
grieved or quenched the Holy Spirit, you can say with great joy,
"I have confessed that sin and I know God has forgiven me and

placing a small red sticker on your pen at work and placing another one
on your bathroom mirror or kitchen refrigerator.

3. As you become more disciplined about confession and cleansing, keep
a journal of the effects on every aspect of your life. If you are married,
how has your marriage been improved? If you are a student, how have
your studies become more diligent? How has Spiritual Breathing helped
you as a parent or child, businessperson or homemaker? I confidently
predict you will see radical growth in every aspect of your life as more
godliness and less sin are evident daily through you.

4. Begin today—right now. Start with a prayer like this: *Lord, I love You and
praise You. I know that You have loved me enough to send Your Son to
die for me, so that every sin I might ever commit will not be held against
me. Here and now, I make this covenant to live a pure and holy life, to
recognize and deal with every sin through immediate confession, and to
repent and grow ever closer to You that You may use me more and more
for Your blessed purposes. I thank You for the wonderful feeling of being
truly clean, truly forgiven, truly adored by the Lord of all creation. Amen.*

cleansed me as He promised." Then leave that sin buried in His forgiveness.

I encourage you to examine your life right now. Are you experiencing the fullness of the Christian life? Are you carrying a load of guilt over past sins in your life? I urge you to begin the process of Spiritual Breathing today. It has helped millions of other Christians, and I know it will also help you.

God's forgiveness is complete. Thank Him for canceling your guilt and cleansing you. Claim victory over those negative feelings and move on in faith to be a fruitful disciple and witness for our Lord.

In with the "good air"!

7

Enjoying God's Grace

I n 1996 I was surprised and humbled to receive a message informing me I had received an honor known as the Templeton Prize. This designation was established in 1971 by Wall Street investor Sir John Templeton to honor those with some unique accomplishment in the field of religion. Among the panel of judges for the 1996 award was President George H. W. Bush, as well as representatives from many of the world's faiths. Mother Teresa, Billy Graham, and Aleksandr Solzhenitsyn were among past honorees. To say the least, it was quite humbling to have my name placed among those of such individuals.

As with any award or form of recognition, I gave all the glory and honor to God. Any praise I receive belongs solely to Him. I would be a fool if I failed to realize, even for a moment, that without Him I would be less than nothing. I happily agreed to accept the honor exclusively for my Savior's glory.

The presentation occurred in London, and the ceremony was held in Rome. A Roman Catholic cardinal was in attendance, along with many other dignitaries, in a very formal and impressive setting. Given this kind of setting, think about what kind of acceptance speech was an appropriate choice on my part. What would you have said? Imagine for a moment that I reached into my pocket, pulled out a five-dollar bill, and said, "That was certainly a fine meal. This feast must have cost somebody a tidy sum of money, so please allow me to chip in my share!"

I would predict there would have been an awkward silence throughout the room at the very least. To offer a few dollars would, of course, be an insult to my eminent hosts. It would have cheapened the wonderful and gracious gesture of the award and the dinner.

> *But the life you live as a result constitutes your acceptance speech. What will you say?*

Now, this would not be true simply because five dollars was a ridiculously insufficient sum; *no* offer of payment would be adequate or appropriate in the face of a such a meaningful—and *priceless*—gift as a world-class award for work in the fields of the kingdom of God. The appropriate response from me was to graciously accept a gracious gift, period. This was one time when it was more blessed to receive!

THE GIFT OF GRACE

Did you notice the key word? *Gracious*, or *grace* for short. A gift of grace has nothing to do with our ability or inability to earn what has been placed before us. It is not connected to any system of conditions other than the necessity of accepting the gift. We simply bow our heads in humility and accept the gift *graciously*.

In the same way, I stand before my God to receive the gift

we have explored in this book: the awesome gift of total for-giveness. He has declared that every misguided action, every poor motive, every unclean thought from my past, my present, or my future is hereby pardoned. When I think about every day and every moment of this long life I have led, I realize the enormity of my failure to live in the holiness and perfection that would meet His standards. To forgive all of my sin—past, present, and future—is a sweeping work of grace whose mag-nitude I cannot comprehend. I cannot pay it back. I cannot do anything but express my gratitude every day of my life and pour out my life as a sacrifice to His wonderful purposes for me and my world.

Think about your own life. How many years have you lived so far? How many moments are there in a life of that many years? Thousands? Millions? During how many seconds, min-utes, and hours have you failed to be the kind of person that a perfect and holy God would have you be? For every misspent second, there is a drop of blood; for every failed moment, a cry of pain from that cruel cross. Our Lord Jesus Christ loves you so much that He took all of the punishment the world could dish out, and if you had been the only person in this world, He would have still done it *just for you*.

That is the designated award, with your name inscribed upon it forever in the halls of eternity. It is a gift so precious it cannot be repaid. But the life you live as a result constitutes your acceptance speech. What will you say?

If you continue toiling and laboring to earn His love, through any goodness of your own—church membership, serv-ice, good deeds, obeying the Ten Commandments—it amounts to reaching into your wallet for a shabby five-dollar bill in the face of the most awesome, powerful, and supernatural gift of love the universe has ever seen. Because this is a gift of *grace*, you cannot deserve it, earn it, or maintain it once you have received it. As a matter of fact, on the very best day of your life you deserve that gift no more than on the worst. It is the same for me and for everyone else.

TOTAL FREEDOM AND JOY

Our efforts mean nothing (in terms of forgiveness); Christ's atonement means everything. Only as Christ continues to stand before the Father, interceding for you and for me, our names written in the scars in His wrists, do we maintain the freedom of this forgiven status.

Yes, of course I will pursue all the good works that come with the Christian life. But I will pursue them for sheer joy and love rather than as a misguided effort to pull my weight and push through those immense heavenly doors. I will pursue my works with the same spirit that is within me when I buy a gift for my wife. I know I cannot earn the devotion she has given me throughout our marriage, but it pleases me to please her. Serving God is that way.

It is a whole new world for you and for me. The old way, trying to pull our own righteous weight, has passed away. The writer of Hebrews tells us about this new way—this new contract we have signed with our Lord:

> "This is the new covenant I will make with my people on that day, says the Lord: I will put my laws in their hearts so they will understand them, and I will write them on their minds so they will obey them."

Then he adds, "I will never again remember their sins and lawless deeds."

Now when sins have been forgiven, there is no need to offer any more sacrifices.

And so, dear brothers and sisters, we can boldly enter heaven's Most Holy Place because of the blood of Jesus.

HEBREWS 10:16–19

This is total forgiveness, and it leads to the life of total freedom and joy. Jesus has promised us, "I have come that they may have life, and that they may have *it* more abundantly" (John 10:10 NKJV). What is that kind of life like?

THE ABUNDANT LIFE

In the light of God's grace, we live before Him to enjoy Him as He enjoys us; to serve Him because, through His Son's sacrifice, He has served us; and to love Him with the greatest passion of our being because He first loved us. We live in fellowship with Him joyfully, boldly, and fearlessly. John writes: "Such love has no fear because perfect love expels all fear. If we are afraid, it is for fear of judgment, and this shows that his love has not been perfected in us. We love each other as a result of his loving us first" (1 John 4:18–19). And now we begin to see the fruit of His grace within and through us: a godly love of others.

LET LOVE OVERFLOW

If you have truly received the gift of God's love and forgiveness, there is no way you can fail to let that love overflow to those around you. The leading indicator, the essential proof of whether or not we are living the life of total forgiveness, is in the demonstration of how we relate to other people. The love of God is not a private experience that can be hoarded, any more than you can hoard the sunshine outdoors on a spring day. It always escapes. It always overflows to those around us. The apostle John put it this way:

> If we love our Christian brothers and sisters, it proves that we have passed from death to eternal life. But a person who has no love is still dead. Anyone who hates another Christian is really a murderer at heart. And you know that murderers don't have eternal life within them. We know what real love is because Christ gave up his life for us. And so we also ought to give up our lives for our Christian brothers and sisters.
>
> 1 JOHN 3:14–16

When you see a person who harbors hatred in his or her heart, you know that person is not living in the light and love of Christ.

FORGIVE—AS GOD FORGIVES YOU

The next mark of a child of grace is our forgiveness of other people. How can we not forgive others when we ourselves have been forgiven of so much? In Matthew 18:21–35, Jesus told a story about a man sentenced to life imprisonment for a colossal financial debt he could not pay. The master decided to forgive the debt and send him home. But as he left, the for-given man saw someone who owed him a much smaller debt, and he demanded immediate repayment. When the earlier, forgiving master heard about this, he recalled the man he had released and imprisoned him again. Jesus concludes, "That's what my heavenly Father will do to you if you refuse to forgive your brothers and sisters in your heart" (verse 35). (See appendix A.)

If you embrace the total forgiveness that Christ has offered you, you will take His love and apply it to everyone you know. You will take His forgiveness and offer it to everyone who wrongs you.

Share Your Faith Joyfully

Finally, the mark of a child of grace is that this person actively shares his or her faith. After truly experiencing the powerful forgiveness of God, we cannot help but love everyone we know, we cannot help but forgive everyone who wrongs us, and

---

Put It to Work

How, then, can you begin to act on the principles of this life of grace? You can take these initial steps:

1. As you worship God daily, use this mental picture of God's gift: You stand before His awesome palace in heaven. All the angels are present, and He sits upon His throne. Your Father tells you that all that He has— every good and perfect spiritual thing—is yours simply because He loves you so much. You cannot offer to pay for that gift in any way. But each day, as you imagine yourself in this setting, you will allow your heart to overflow with love and gratitude for such a loving Father. And you will live that day as your "acceptance speech."

2. Spend time thanking God and praying something like this: *Precious Lord, what an incredible joy to anticipate the new life I look forward to leading as a child of grace and total forgiveness. As You have loved me, I cannot wait to go and love others! As You have forgiven me, I am eager to forgive every wrong that has been done to me or will be done to me. And as You rescued me from eternal judgment and a life of despair and meaninglessness, my heart is filled with a desire for You to use me in bringing that same wonderful gift to others. I am Yours to use as You will, dear Lord. Amen.*

---

we cannot help but share our faith with everyone who lives in darkness.

Before Jesus left this earth to sit at the right hand of His Father in heaven, He said, "But when the Holy Spirit has come upon you, you will receive power and will tell people about me everywhere ... to the ends of the earth" (Acts 1:8). Again, there is no optional element indicated by that verse. When we accept the lordship and forgiveness of Christ, the Holy Spirit comes to live within us. His overarching agenda is that each one of us be used to lead lost people to the same wonderful discovery we have made.

※

These, then, are just a few of the marks of a child of grace—a person who has totally embraced the love and forgiveness that our Father has offered us through the death and resurrection of His Son. Love, forgiveness, and faith sharing will grow naturally and joyfully from your life out of the overflow of gracious fellowship you enjoy with your Lord.

How wonderful it is to know that this life of faith is a life of abundance—a life to be enjoyed. It is a life not of slavish toiling to please a tyrannical master, but one of loving friendship with a Father who has chosen to make us His children in every sense, so that we have all the spiritual riches and privileges of His kingdom. All of our sins have been neutralized by the death of Christ on the cross. We will continue to stumble, of course, but through Spiritual Breathing and the accountability of our fellow Christians, as well as the daily guidance of the Holy Spirit, we will look a bit more like our Savior every day.

8

Abiding in God's Freedom

There is a rather amusing old legend about the town of Duckville, USA. It is more than a bit silly, but I ask you to bear with me as I relate it—there is nothing silly about its message.

In Duckville, USA, the ducks live in houses built of mud. These homes are a bit crude and smelly. They are not the best or most comfortable of residences, but they are the most adequate shelter the ducks can figure out how to build. They eat mostly small bugs that happen to fly through the windows, and they try to keep warm when the winter breezes whistle through those windows.

On the other hand, these ducks do have a very nice church building that someone managed to build for them. It has stood for many duck generations. This great facility is as attractive as any church you would find in any town, and the ducks just love congregating there on weekends.

Every Sunday morning, the ducks emerge from their duck homes. They come waddling down Mallard Lane until they reach their church. Arranging themselves comfortably in their pews, they enjoy the music of the all-duck choir. They quack a few hymns, then the duck preacher waddles up to the podium and delivers a powerful sermon. The ducks look forward to the sermon all week. Its message is generally the same: "My friends, be joyful! Be thankful! For good news is upon us, and that news is that you are ducks!" He goes on, "Brothers and sisters, as ducks, you are very special birds. You are built for the water, and you have the wonderful gift of webbed feet that allow you to swim beautifully. And you have a long beak that allows you to take hold of an absolutely terrific food. They call it *fish!* This fish is so much tastier, so much more filling and nutritious than the meager gnats and flies of which you have all grown so weary. All you have to do is swim out there on the water, and you will find yourself surrounded by lovely, delectable fish of every kind."

———❖———

All we need to do is accept the total forgiveness He has offered, then allow His Spirit to live within us every day.

———

The duck preacher continues his sermon, building in intensity. "There is even more good news!" he quacks resoundingly. "You can *fly*—each one of you! Do you realize what that means? You were given strong and glorious wings, so that you can fly to the four corners of the earth and find all the water and all the fish you could ever eat! And when it gets cold, my fine-feathered friends, you need not shiver in your mud hut; you can fly to a warmer place where all the really intelligent ducks take their winter vacations. And when danger comes, you can flap those wings and fly to safety. Brothers and sisters, I want to see every one of you flap those wings!" And with that, the sanctuary is filled with flapping, quacking, and honking.

At the end of the sermon, all the ducks come waddling

down the aisle to thank the reverend for his inspiring sermon. They quack happily together before waddling back up the aisle, out the door, down Mallard Lane again, and back to their mud huts to resume shivering until next week. And so life goes on in Duckville, USA.

WALK THE WALK

We can have a good laugh over that very silly story, but the truth in it is all too recognizable. Like the poor birds of that town, we do a lot of quacking—er, *talking*—about our faith. We hear sermons about it and become very excited. We listen to lovely music about the supernatural life. But when the time comes for living out our faith—"walking the walk"—many of us are more than a bit like ducks out of water. We waddle when we could be flying, and we nibble gnats when we could be feasting from God's table.

Let us think about what life would be like if we lived abundantly in the light of God's total love and forgiveness, as the Word of God plainly tells us we can live.

Here is a picture of the supernatural life—the realization of total forgiveness—as it is meant to be lived:

> He gives power to those who are tired and worn out; he
> offers strength to the weak. Even youths will become
> exhausted, and young men will give up. But those who wait
> on the LORD will find new strength. They will fly high on
> wings like eagles. They will run and not grow weary. They
> will walk and not faint.
>
> ISAIAH 40:29–31

Ducks are never mentioned in the Bible, for we are to soar

like eagles. God built us for freedom. He wants us to touch the clouds and dominate the horizon of this ailing world. All we need to do is accept the total forgiveness He has offered, then allow His Spirit to live within us every day. It is that simple. "But we who live by the Spirit eagerly wait to receive everything promised to us who are right with God through faith" (Galatians 5:5). There is no end to the abundance of good things that our gracious and generous Lord brings to the table when we join that great feast. For appetizers, check the menu of the fruit of the Spirit found later in that same fifth chapter from Galatians:

> But when the Holy Spirit controls our lives, he will produce this kind of fruit in us: love, joy, peace, patience, kindness, goodness, faithfulness, gentleness, and self-control.
>
> GALATIANS 5:22–23

Just thinking about such delectable fruit is what I call a foretaste of glory divine! It is just the beginning of the abundant life that the Lord Jesus Christ wants you to have every single day, on into eternity when you will remain in His loving presence forever. Each of those fruits—love, joy, peace, and all the rest—will ripen and become more sweet, more lovely in your life, every day that you keep in step with the Spirit. Across the years, He plans to enhance each of those traits until you become a living replica of our Savior. This

Across the years, He plans to enhance each of those traits until you become a living replica of our Savior. This has been His plan all along.

has been His plan all along: "For God knew his people in advance, and he chose them to become like his Son, so that his Son would be the firstborn, with many brothers and sisters" (Romans 8:29).

DEATH TO SIN

We may intellectually grasp the concept of physical death, but we have not fully comprehended the fact that our sins are *spiritually* dead—buried and gone. Micah 7:19 promises us that our God "will trample our sins under [His] feet and throw them into the depths of the ocean!" Hebrews 8:12 offers God's assurance to His people that He "will forgive their wrongdoings, and … will never again remember their sins."

How many more ways need it be explained to us? As far as God is concerned, if we have chosen Christ as our Lord and Savior, our sins are just plain gone. My friend, that is bigger news than any event in human history. It has more implications for your life than any other single fact we could be discussing. To take hold of its full implications will turn your life, and your world, upside down. Heaven is a very real place where we look forward to seeing God face to face, but God's most devoted servants have discovered that paradise actually begins right here, right now, the very moment we decide to let the old way of life die and let the Holy Spirit take hold of us completely.

As we close this book, let us preview your future as a free, forgiven child of God, ready to be all that He intends you to be.

———————❖———————

"ABIDE IN ME, AND I IN YOU. AS THE BRANCH
CANNOT BEAR FRUIT OF ITSELF, UNLESS IT
ABIDES IN THE VINE, NEITHER CAN YOU,
UNLESS YOU ABIDE IN ME.
I AM THE VINE, YOU ARE THE BRANCHES.
HE WHO ABIDES IN ME, AND I IN HIM,
BEARS MUCH FRUIT; FOR WITHOUT ME
YOU CAN DO NOTHING."

—JESUS CHRIST

————————————

$\overline{\underset{\overline{}}{9}}$

Live It!

One of the most wonderful words in our beloved, inerrant Scripture is the word *abide*. It means to remain somewhere, but it has the additional meaning of awaiting or expecting. Here is how our Lord and Savior used the word:

> "Abide in Me, and I in you. As the branch cannot bear fruit of itself, unless it abides in the vine, neither can you, unless you abide in Me. I am the vine, you are the branches. He who abides in Me, and I in him, bears much fruit; for without Me you can do nothing."
>
> JOHN 15:4–5 NKJV

We have discussed some of the wonderful fruit of the life of total forgiveness, but it is also true that we ourselves are like the fruit of the vine. We are connected to Christ in that same exclusive way. We draw all our life, all our vitality and spiritual lifeblood, from Him—as long as we stay connected. And as Christ flows into us, we live also "in Him."

It is worth stopping to meditate upon that powerful idea. Just turning your mind and spirit toward this idea every day, for a reflective moment, is enough to completely change your life. The truth is that you are free from all the sin and failure in this world that would enslave you. You are free, as we have seen, to love, to forgive, and to experience the unmatched joy of sharing your faith with others. You are free to explore the unique spiritual gifts the Holy Spirit has given you. You are free to pursue the wonderful plans that God has designed for you, and only you, since the foundation of the universe. You are free to enjoy loving fellowship with your Savior every day of your life

PUT IT TO WORK

What steps can you take to connect to Christ, the true vine, today?

1. Spend time in prayer reflecting on what it means to be a branch of the true vine (John 15:4–5). What should be the vital signs that you are abiding in Him? What would it mean to "ripen" and what fruit does He wish you to produce? In practical terms, what behavior in yourself would reflect your connection to Christ?

2. Over the next few days, review each of the chapters in this book. Write down the most life-changing concept you gathered from each one. Review the exercises you performed in the final sections and create a specific plan to follow through with these disciplines in the future. For example, how will you continue to claim the forgiveness you have learned about? How will you make Spiritual Breathing a vital part of your daily experience?

3. Our Lord wants you to soar like an eagle, to run and not grow weary (Isaiah 40:29–31). Reflect upon one area in your life where you have grown weary and need the supernatural power of Christ to help you soar. Stop and claim His promise that you can live in the power of His Spirit in this area. What changes will you make? What victories can be claimed?

4. In reflecting upon the message of total forgiveness, how are you better able to forgive? How will you practice the gift of grace in the future? Who do you most need to forgive—parents? Coworkers? God? Yourself?

and everywhere you go. He has promised He will never leave nor forsake you (Hebrews 13:5). You are free from the fear of death, because you know that to live is Christ and to die is gain—you will see your Father face to face (Philippians 1:21).

Total forgiveness means abiding in every precious and liberating freedom of Christ, particularly the freedom to remain in Christ as He remains in you, as He promised His disciples as a parting gift on that last night together in the Upper Room. What a gift! No legacy could be more precious; no joy could be more profound; no love could be more powerful.

Forgive by faith, and act upon your covenant. You might need to tell these people you have forgiven them. You might find a way to serve them, so that God will increase your love for them (see appendix A).

5. Ask God to use you to share the message of this book and the full message of salvation through Christ, actively. Ask Him to start with one person to whom you can speak. God has promised to answer this prayer, so expect Him to use you immediately to share the message of total forgiveness with a wounded, confused world that so deeply craves it.

The blessings of God will go with you, the love of Christ will uphold you, and the comfort of the Spirit will bolster you as He sends you forth on the greatest adventure life can offer! You might offer this prayer of thanksgiving as you set out on the journey:

Gracious heavenly Father, my heart is full with the wonder of Your gift and the fullness of Your grace. I go forth now to live in the freedom and power of total forgiveness. I go forth to offer love and redemption as surely as they have been offered to me. I go forth in Your power to cast out darkness as surely as it has been cast out from the corners of my soul. I go forth to offer living water to the thirsty, just as it has already quenched my own thirst. I will abide in You, even as You abide in me. I thank You and praise You for the victory of all victories! Amen.

TO EACH OF US

As I look out upon the crowds of a busy street in this modern-day world, I think about this staggering fact: every single face in that sea of humanity has been offered this gift. The gift of total forgiveness is available to each man, woman, and child in this world—6.5 billion people, all eligible for the greatest gift that could ever be given. The great heartbeat of my life has been for God to use me to let every single one of them have the opportunity to accept the gift and be freed from the terrible, destructive burden of sin that bears down upon every person in that crowd on the city street, every person in your city, every living inhabitant of our world.

> *The love and forgiveness and freedom of Christ are simply too precious to horde; they must be shared.*

I want to close by revealing to you the one final step you can take to fully enjoy the abundance and freedom of all that Christ offers. That is the step of telling others about the joy you have discovered. You might give this book to a friend who desperately needs it. You might use the resources in this and other books in this series to help you learn to share your faith. You might begin to pray every day for a fresh opportunity to bring another of the children our Savior died for into His loving arms.

As wonderful as the transforming life of total forgiveness is, I have discovered that it is never complete unless we are actively telling others about it as well. For that is God's own heartbeat. That is the overarching purpose He has reserved for all His beloved. The love and forgiveness and freedom of Christ are simply too precious to horde; they must be shared.

Whose face has the Spirit of God brought to the surface of your reflections? To whom is He sending you on a rescue mission? A great joy—life's deepest—awaits you, and my prayers go with you. May the total forgiveness of God bring about a life of total service for you.

Readers' Guide

For Personal Reflection or Group Discussion

Questions are an inevitable part of life. Proud parents ask their new baby, "Can you smile?" Later they ask, "Can you say 'Mama'?" "Can you walk to Daddy?" The early school years bring the inevitable, "What did you learn at school today?" Later school years introduce tougher questions, "If X equals 12 and Y equals –14, then …?" Adulthood adds a whole new set of questions. "Should I remain single or marry?" "How did things go at the office?" "Did you get a raise?" "Should we let Susie start dating?" "Which college is right for Kyle?" "How can we possibly afford to send our kids to college?"

This book raises questions too. The following study guide is designed to (1) maximize the subject material and (2) apply biblical truth to daily life. You won't be asked to solve any algebraic problems or recall dates associated with obscure events in history, so relax. Questions asking for objective information are based solely on the text. Most questions, however, prompt you to search inside your soul, examine the circumstances that surround your life, and decide how you can best use the truths communicated in the book.

Honest answers to real issues can strengthen your faith, draw you closer to the Lord, and lead you into fuller, richer, more joyful, and productive daily adventures. So confront each question head-on and expect the One who is the answer for all of life's questions and needs to accomplish great things in your life.

CHAPTER 1: DESIRING GOD'S FORGIVENESS

1. In what sense is every human being a prodigal son or daughter?

2. What religious endeavors suggest that human beings long for forgiveness? How effective are those endeavors in erasing guilt? Explain your answer.

3. Why do you agree or disagree that the person brought up to attend church regularly and to lead a respectable life needs forgiveness as much as the person who leads a pagan lifestyle?

4. Have you experienced God's forgiveness? If you have, what circumstances led to this forgiveness?

5. Why can our heavenly Father freely forgive whoever seeks His forgiveness?

CHAPTER 2: RECEIVING GOD'S FORGIVENESS

1. How was the substitutionary death of Jesus Christ adequate payment for all your sins?

2. How would you answer someone who insists that Christ's death was the basis of forgiveness for past sins only?

3. How does the belief that forgiveness comes exclusively through Jesus contradict the popular philosophy known as pluralism?

4. Does a person have to feel forgiven to be forgiven? Why or why not?

5. What analogies might highlight the vast distance that exists between our sinfulness and God's righteousness? How does an awareness of this distance deepen your appreciation of reconciliation?

CHAPTER 3: PURSUING GOD'S HEART

1. How do you define "repentance"? What role, if any, does repentance play in forgiveness?

2. Read Psalm 32 and list six words that describe how King David felt before God forgave him.

3. What difference or differences do you see between punishment and discipline?

4. How can a believer emerge stronger than ever after receiving God's forgiveness for moral failure?

5. Define "confession," as it appears in 1 John 1:9. What does genuine confession accomplish in the life of a believer?

CHAPTER 4: EXPERIENCING GOD'S CLEANSING

1. How difficult is it to do the right thing in the workplace? Why should Christians always to do the right thing?

2. How do you think most nonbelievers regard Christians who do the right thing?

3. How does sinning on the part of believers crucify Christ anew?

4. We cannot lead a sinless life, but what can we do to live as free of sin as possible?

5. How does the author link "Spiritual Breathing" and confession?

CHAPTER 5: SPIRITUAL BREATHING

1. Why do you agree or disagree that sin obstructs communication with God?

2. Can we distinguish between "little sins" and "big sins"? Why or why not?

3. How do unconfessed sins gather momentum?

4. Confessing sins means to agree with God about them. If you were to receive an agreement form from God, what would you expect to see listed on the form?

5. What sins do you think most Christians would list if they prepared such a list of sins to confess to God? Which of these sins do you need to confess? Which of the sins require restitution?

CHAPTER 6: FORGIVEN ONCE AND FOR ALL

1. How fully does God forgive sin? Cite two Scripture passages that support your answer.

2. What should a believer do when he or she feels tempted to dredge up sins God has buried in the sea of His forgetfulness?

3. How does the assurance that all your sins are forgiven forever empower you to share the good news with others?

4. How might a journal about one's spiritual progress encourage a person to confess sins promptly?

5. How are genuine love for God and love of sinning mutually exclusive?

CHAPTER 7: ENJOYING GOD'S GRACE

1. How does God reveal His grace when He forgives sins?

2. If a nonbeliever asked you to explain the meaning of grace, how would you respond?

3. Why do you agree or disagree that it is impossible to earn God's love?

4. What value do you attach to good works performed to earn salvation? What value do you attach to good works performed to show gratitude for salvation?

5. In what tangible ways does love flow from a grateful heart?

CHAPTER 8: ABIDING IN GOD'S FREEDOM

1. What do you think it might take to transport twenty-first century believers to a higher level of Christianity?

2. Do you agree or disagree that a Christian may possess some qualities listed as the fruit of the Spirit in Galatians 5:22, 23 but lack the others? Defend your answer.

3. How has someone you observed manifested the fruit of the Spirit?

4. Which of the following descriptions best identifies the state of our sins: (a) dying, (b) sentenced to death, (c) dead? Defend your choice.

5. What does it mean to let the old way of life die? What might result in your community if most Christians let their old way of life die?

CHAPTER 9: LIVE IT!

1. How does awareness of total forgiveness liberate a believer?

2. How does knowing the liberating power of total forgiveness motivate you to share your faith?

3. How do you distinguish between being in Christ and abiding in Christ?

4. In what ways might believers touch their community with God's love?

5. With whom will you share God's love this week? How will you pray as you anticipate sharing God's love?

——————❖——————

CHRIST LOVES YOU SO MUCH THAT, WHILE YOU
WERE A SINNER, HE DIED FOR YOU.

——————————

Appendix A

How to Love by Faith

The beautiful ballroom of the Marriott Hotel in Chicago was crowded to capacity with more than 1,300 college students and Campus Crusade staff. They seemed to hang on to every word as I explained one of the most exciting spiritual discoveries that I had ever made—how to love by faith.

For years I had spoken on the subject of love. I had a simple four-point outline:

1. God loves you unconditionally.
2. You are commanded to love others—God, your neighbors, your enemies.
3. You are incapable of loving others in your own strength.
4. You can love others with God's love.

But, as in the case of most sermons on love, something was missing. Then, in an early hour of the morning, I was awakened from a deep sleep. I felt impressed to get up, open my Bible, and kneel to read and pray. What I discovered during the next two hours has since enriched my life and the lives of tens of thousands of others. I had learned how to love.

In that life-changing time of fellowship with the Lord, I

was given a fifth point for my sermon on love—we love *by faith*.

Love is the greatest thing in the world—the greatest privilege and power known to man. Its practice in word and deed changed the course of history as the first-century Christians demonstrated a quality of life never before witnessed on this earth. The Greeks, Romans, Gentiles, and Jews hated one another. The very idea of love and self-sacrifice was foreign to their thinking. When they observed Christians from many nations, with different languages and cultures, actually loving one another and sacrificing to help each other, they responded in amazement, "Look how these Christians love one another!"

> *Love is the greatest thing in the world—the greatest privilege and power known to man.*

I challenged the students at the conference to become part of a revolution of love. I suggested that they make a list of all the individuals they did not like and begin to love them by faith.

Early the next morning, a young woman with face aglow said to me, "My life was changed last night. For many years I have hated my parents. I haven't seen them since I was seventeen, and I am now twenty-two. I left home as a result of a quarrel five years ago and haven't written or talked to them since, although they have repeatedly encouraged me to return home. I determined that I would never see them again. I hated them.

"Before becoming a Christian a few months ago," she continued, "I had become a drug addict, a dope pusher, and a prostitute. Last night you told me how to love my parents, and I could hardly wait to get out of that meeting and call them. Can you believe it? I now really love them with God's kind of love and can hardly wait to see them!"

Everybody wants to be loved. Most psychologists agree that man's greatest need is to love and be loved. No barrier can withstand the mighty force of love.

There are three Greek words translated into the one English word "love":

> *Eros*, which suggests sensual desire—it does not appear in the New Testament.
>
> *Phileo*, which is used for friendship or love of one's friends or relatives—it conveys a sense of loving someone because he is worthy of love.
>
> *Agape*, which is God's love: the purest, deepest kind of love—it is expressed not through mere emotions but as an act of one's will.

Agape is God's supernatural, unconditional love for you revealed supremely through our Lord's death on the cross for your sins. It is the supernatural love He wants to produce in you and through you to others, by His Holy Spirit. *Agape* love is given because of the character of the person loving rather than because of the worthiness of the object of that love. Sometimes it is love "in spite of" rather than "because of."

God underscores the importance of this kind of love through the inspired writing of the apostle Paul, as recorded in 1 Corinthians 13. In this beautiful and remarkable passage of Scripture, Paul writes that, apart from love, anything that you might do for God or others is of no value. Consider these words:

> If I had the gift of being able to speak in other languages without learning them, and could speak in every language

there is in all of heaven and earth, but didn't love others,
I would only be making noise. If I had the gift of
prophecy and knew all about what is going to happen in
the future, knew everything about *everything*, but didn't
love others, what good would it do? Even if I had the gift
of faith so that I could speak to a mountain and make it
move, I would still be worth nothing at all without love. If
I gave everything I have to poor people, and if I were
burned alive for preaching the Gospel but didn't love
others, it would be of no value whatever.

1 CORINTHIANS 13:1–3 TLB

In other words, no matter what you do for God and for others, it is of no value unless you are motivated by God's love.

FIVE TRUTHS ABOUT LOVE

But what is *agape* love? How does this kind of love express itself? Paul gives us an excellent description:

Love is very patient and kind, never jealous or envious,
never boastful or proud, never haughty or selfish or rude.
Love does not demand its own way. It is not irritable or
touchy. It does not hold grudges and will hardly even
notice when others do it wrong. It is never glad about
injustice, but rejoices whenever truth wins out. If you
love someone you will be loyal to him no matter what the
cost. You will always believe in him, always expect the
best of him, and always stand your ground in defending
him.

All the special gifts and powers from God will
someday come to an end, but love goes on forever....

There are three things that remain—faith, hope, and
love—and the greatest of these is love.

1 CORINTHIANS 13:4–8, 13 TLB

In the next chapter the apostle Paul, inspired by the Holy
Spirit, admonishes: "Let love be your greatest aim" (1
Corinthians 14:1 TLB).

Let me share with you five vital truths about love that will
help you understand the basis for loving by faith.

1. GOD LOVES YOU UNCONDITIONALLY

God loves with *agape* love, the love described in 1
Corinthians 13. He loves you so much that He sent His Son
to die on the cross for you so that you might have everlasting
life. His love is not based on performance. Christ loves you so
much that, while you were yet a sin-
ner, He died for you.

God's love for you is unconditional and undeserved. He loves you
in spite of your disobedience, your
weakness, your sin, and your selfish-

> *God's love for you is
> unconditional and
> undeserved.*

ness. He loves you enough to provide a way to abundant,
eternal life. From the cross Christ cried out, "Father, forgive
them, for they do not know what they are doing" (Luke 23:34
NIV). If God loved those who are sinners that much, can you
imagine how much He loves you—His child through faith in
Christ and who seeks to please Him?

God demonstrated His love for us before we were
Christians, but the parable of the prodigal son (Luke 15)

makes it obvious that God continues to love His child who has strayed far from Him. He eagerly awaits his return to the Christian family and fellowship.

Even when you are disobedient, He continues to love you, waiting for you to respond to His love and forgiveness. Paul writes:

> Since by his blood he did all this for us as sinners, how much more will he do for us now that he has declared us not guilty? Now he will save us from all of God's wrath to come. And since, when we were his enemies, we were brought back to God by the death of his Son, what blessings he must have for us now that we are his friends and he is living within us!
>
> ROMAN 5:9–10 TLB

The love that God has for you is far beyond our human comprehension. Jesus prayed, "My prayer for all of them [the disciples and all future believers] is that they will be of one heart and mind, just as you and I are, Father … I in them and you in me, all being perfected into one—so that the world will know you sent me and will understand that you love them as much as you love me" (John 17:21, 23 TLB).

Think of it! God loves you as much as He loves His only begotten Son … What a staggering, overwhelming truth to comprehend.

Think of it! God loves you as much as He loves His only begotten Son, the Lord Jesus. What a staggering, overwhelming truth to comprehend! You need have no fear of someone who loves you perfectly. You need never be reluctant to trust God with your entire life, for He truly loves you. And the almost unbelievable part of it is that He loves you even when you are disobedient.

2. YOU ARE COMMANDED TO LOVE GOD AND OTHERS

A certain lawyer asked Jesus, "Sir, which is the most important command in the laws of Moses?"

Jesus replied, "'Love the Lord your God with all your heart, soul, and mind.' This is the first and greatest commandment. The second most important is similar: 'Love your neighbor as much as you love yourself.' All the other commandments and all the demands of the prophets stem from these two laws and are fulfilled if you obey them. Keep only these and you will find that you are obeying all the others" (Matthew 22:37–40 TLB).

At one time in my Christian life, I was troubled over the command to love God so completely. How could I ever measure up to such a high standard? Two very important considerations have helped me to desire to love and please Him completely.

First, the Holy Spirit has filled my heart with God's love, as promised in Romans:

> We know how dearly God loves us, and we feel this warm
> love everywhere within us because God has given us the
> Holy Spirit to fill our hearts with his love.
>
> ROMANS 5:5 TLB

Second, by meditating on the attributes of God and the wonderful things He has done and is doing for me, I find my love for Him growing. I love Him because He first loved me (1 John 4:19).

How could God love me so much that He was willing to die for me? Why should God choose me to be His child? By what merit do I deserve to be His ambassador to tell this good news of His love and forgiveness to the world? On what basis do I deserve the privilege of His constant presence and His indwelling Spirit, of His promise to supply all of my needs according to His riches in glory? Why should I have the privilege—denied to most of the people of the world who do not know our Savior—of awaking each morning with a song in my heart and praise to Him on my lips for the love and joy and peace that He so generously gives to all who place their trust in His dear Son, the Lord Jesus?

You are commanded to love others because such love testifies to your relationship with the Father. You demonstrate that you belong to Christ by your love for others.

The one who has not yet learned to love God and to seek Him above all else and all others is to be pitied, for that person is missing the blessings that await all who love God with all of their hearts, souls, and minds.

It is natural for you to fulfill the command to love your neighbors as yourself if you truly love God with all of your heart, soul, and mind. If you are properly related to God on the vertical plane, you will be properly related to others on the horizontal plane.

For example, billiard balls, rolling freely on a table, naturally bounce away from each other because of the nature of their construction. But if we tie strings to several balls and lift them perpendicular to the table, the balls will cluster together.

When individual Christians are vitally yoked to Christ and related to God and are walking in the Spirit, loving Him with all of their hearts, souls, and minds, they will fulfill God's command to love others as themselves.

The apostle Paul explains:

> If you love your neighbor as much as you love yourself
> you will not want to harm or cheat him, or kill him or
> steal from him. And you won't sin with his wife or want
> what is his, or do anything else the Ten Commandments
> say is wrong. All ten are wrapped up in this one, to love
> your neighbor as you love yourself. Love does no wrong
> to anyone. That's why it fully satisfies all of God's require-
> ments. It is the only law you need.
>
> ROMANS 13:9–10 TLB

It is love for God and for others that results in righteous-ness, in fruit, and in glory to Christ.

Also, you are commanded to love others because such love testifies to your relationship with the Father. You demonstrate that you belong to Christ by your love for oth-ers. The apostle John practically equates your salvation with the way you love others when he says that if you don't love others, you do not know God, for He is love.

> If someone who is supposed to be a Christian has money
> enough to live well, and sees a brother in need, and
> won't help him—how can God's love be within *him*?
> Little children, let us stop just *saying* we love people; let
> us *really* love them, and *show it* by our *actions*.
>
> 1 JOHN 3:17–18 TLB

Jesus says: "I demand that you love each other as much as I love you" (John 15:12 TLB).

As a Christian, you should love your neighbor because your neighbor is a creature of God made in the image of God, because God loves your neighbor, and because Christ died for your neighbor. Following the example of our Lord, you should love everyone, even as Christ did. You should devote your life to helping others experience His love and forgiveness. Jesus also said:

> *"God loves you and accepts you as you are. You must do the same."*

> "There is a saying, 'Love your *friends* and hate your enemies.' But I say: Love your *enemies*! Pray for those who *persecute* you! In that way you will be acting as true sons of your Father in heaven.... If you love only those who love you, what good is that? Even scoundrels do that much. If you are friendly only to your friends, how are you different from anyone else? Even the heathen do that."
>
> MATTHEW 5:43–47 TLB

When Christians begin to act like Christians and love God, their neighbors, their enemies, and especially their Christian brothers—regardless of color, race, or class—we will see in our time, as in the first century, a great transformation in the whole of society. People will marvel when they observe our love in the same way people marveled when they observed those first-century believers, saying, "How they love one another!"

I counsel many students and older adults who are not able to accept themselves. Some are weighted down with guilt because of unconfessed sins; others are not reconciled to their physical handicaps; still others feel inferior mentally or socially. My counsel to one and all is, "God loves you and accepts you as you are. You must do the same. Get your eyes off yourself! Focus your love and attention on Christ and on others. Begin to lose yourself in service for Him and for your fellow man."

God's kind of love is a unifying force among Christians. Paul admonishes us to *"put on* love, which is the perfect bond of unity" (Colossians 3:14 NASB) that our "hearts may be encouraged, having been knit together in love" (Colossians 2:2 NASB). Only God's universal love can break through the troublesome barriers that are created by human differences. Only a common devotion to Christ—the source of love—can relieve tension, ease mistrust, encourage openness, bring out the best in people, and enable them to serve Christ together in a more fruitful way.

One mother shared that the discovery of these principles enabled her to be more patient and kind to her husband and children. "The children were driving me out of my mind with all of their childish demands," she confided. "I was irritable with them, and because I was so miserable, I was a critical and nagging wife. No wonder my husband found excuses to work late at the office. It is all different now—God's love permeates our home since I learned how to love by faith."

A husband reported, "My wife and I have fallen in love all over again, and I am actually enjoying working in my office with men I couldn't stand before I learned how to love by faith."

3. You Cannot Love in Your Own Strength

Just as surely as "those who are in the flesh [the worldly, carnal person] cannot please God," so in your own strength you cannot love as you should.

You cannot demonstrate *agape* love, God's unconditional love for others, through your own efforts. How many times have you resolved to love someone? How often have you tried to manufacture some kind of positive, loving emotion toward another person for whom you felt nothing? It is impossible, isn't it? In your own strength it is not possible to love with God's kind of love.

By nature people are not patient and kind. We are jealous, envious, and boastful. We are proud, haughty, selfish, and rude, and we demand our own way. We could never love others the way God loves us!

4. You Can Love with God's Love

It was God's kind of love that brought you to Christ. It is this kind of love that is able to sustain and encourage you each day. Through His love in you, you can bring others to Christ and minister to fellow believers as God has commanded.

God's love was supremely expressed in the life of Jesus Christ. You have a perfect, complete picture of God's kind of love in the birth, character, teachings, life, death, and resurrection of His Son.

How does this love enter your life? It becomes yours the moment you receive Jesus Christ, and the Holy Spirit comes to indwell your life. The Scripture says, "We feel this warm love everywhere within us because God has given us the Holy Spirit to fill our hearts with his love" (Romans 5:5 TLB). God is Spirit and the "fruit of the Spirit is love ..." (Galatians 5:22 NIV). When you are controlled by the Spirit, you can love with God's love.

When Christ comes into your life and you become a Christian, God gives you the resources to be a different kind of person. With the motivation, He also gives you the ability. He provides you with a new kind of love.

But how do you make love a practical reality in your life? How do you love? By resolutions? By self-imposed discipline? No. The only way to love is explained in my final point.

5. YOU LOVE BY FAITH

Everything about the Christian life is based on faith. You love by faith just as you received Christ by faith, just as you are filled with the Holy Spirit by faith, and just as you walk by faith.

He would not command you to do something that He will not enable you to do.

If the fruit of the Spirit is love, you may logically ask, "Is it not enough to be filled with the Spirit?" This will be true from God's point of view, but it will not always be true in your actual experience.

Many Christians have loved with God's love and have demonstrated the fruit of the Spirit in their lives without consciously or specifically claiming His love by faith. Yet, without being aware of the fact, they were indeed loving by faith; therefore, they did not find it necessary to claim God's love by faith as a specific act.

Hebrews 11:6 says, "Without faith it is impossible to

please God" (NIV). Obviously there will be no demonstration of God's love where there is no faith.

If you have difficulty loving others, remember that Jesus has commanded, "Love each other just as much as I love you" (John 13:34 TLB). It is God's will for you to love. He would not command you to do something that He will not enable you to do. In 1 John 5:14–15, God promises that if you ask anything according to His will, He hears and answers you. Relating this promise to God's command, you can claim by faith the privilege of loving with His love.

> *God has an unending supply of His divine, supernatural* agape *love for you.*

God has an unending supply of His divine, supernatural *agape* love for you. It is for you to claim, to grow on, to spread to others, and thus to reach hundreds and thousands with the love that counts, the love that will bring them to Jesus Christ.

In order to experience and share this love, you must claim it by faith; that is, trust His promise that He will give you all that you need to do His will on the basis of His command and promise.

This truth is not new. It has been recorded in God's Word for 2,000 years. But it was a new discovery to me that early morning some years ago and, since that time, to many thousands of other Christians with whom I have shared it. When I began to practice loving by faith, I found that problems of tension with other individuals seemed to disappear, often miraculously.

In one instance, I was having a problem loving a fellow staff member. It troubled me. I wanted to love him. I knew that I was commanded to love him; yet, because of certain areas of inconsistency and personality differences, it was difficult for me to love him. But the Lord reminded me of 1 Peter 5:7, "Let him have all your worries and cares, for he is always thinking about you and watching everything that concerns you" (TLB). I decided to give this problem to Him and *love this man by faith*. When I claimed God's love for the man by faith, my concern lifted. I knew the matter was in God's hands.

An hour later, I found under my door a letter from that very man, who had no possible way of knowing what I had just experienced. In fact, his letter had been written the day before. The Lord had foreseen the change in me. This friend and I met together that afternoon and had the most wonderful time of prayer and fellowship we had ever experienced together. Loving with God's love by faith has changed our relationship.

Two gifted attorneys had great professional animosity, even hatred one for the other. Even though they were distinguished members of the same firm, they were constantly criticizing and making life miserable for each other.

One of the men received Christ through our ministry and some months later came for counsel.

"I have hated and criticized my partner for years," he said, "and he has been equally antagonistic toward me. But now that I am a Christian, I don't feel right about continuing our warfare. What shall I do?"

"Why not ask your partner to forgive you and tell him that you love him?" I suggested.

"I could never do that!" he exclaimed. "That would be

hypocritical. I don't love him. How could I tell him I love him when I don't?"

I explained that God commands His children to love even their enemies and that His supernatural, unconditional *agape* love is an expression of our will, which we exercise by faith.

For example, the 1 Corinthians 13 kind of love is "very patient and kind, never jealous or envious, never boastful or proud, never haughty or selfish or rude. Love does not demand its own way. It is not irritable or touchy. It does not hold grudges and will hardly even notice when others do it wrong. It is never glad about injustice, but rejoices whenever truth wins out. If you love someone you will be loyal to him no matter what the cost. You will always believe in him, always expect the best of him, and always stand your ground in defending him" (1 Corinthians 13:4–7 TLB).

"You will note," I explained, "that each of these descriptions of love is not an expression of the emotions, but of the will."

Together we knelt to pray and my friend asked God's forgiveness for his critical attitude toward his law partner and claimed God's love for him by faith.

Early the next morning, my friend walked into his partner's office and announced, "Something wonderful has happened to me. I have become a Christian. And I have come to ask you to forgive me for all that I have done to hurt you in the past, and to tell you that I love you."

His partner was so surprised and convicted of his own sin that he responded to this amazing confession by asking my friend to forgive him. Then to my friend's surprise, his partner said, "I would like to become a Christian too. Would you show me what I need to do?"

After my friend showed him how, using a booklet we publish titled *The Four Spiritual Laws*. They knelt together to pray, then they both came to tell me of this marvelous miracle of God's love.

LIBERATED FROM HATE

A young college football player, who had been raised in a community where blacks are resented, had always found it impossible to love blacks. One evening he heard me talk to a group of racially mixed students about loving by faith, especially in reference to loving those of other races.

"As you prayed," he told me later, "I claimed God's love for black people. Then, as I left the amphitheater, the first person I saw was a black man, and he was talking to a white girl. Now that is about as explosive a situation as you can imagine for a man who hates blacks. But suddenly I felt a compassion for that black man! At one time, I would have hated him and probably would have been rude and angry with him. But God heard my prayer."

> *This love is contagious, attractive, and aggressive. It creates hunger for God.*

That same evening a young black couple approached me. They were radiant.

"Something wonderful happened to me tonight," the young woman said. "I was liberated from my hatred for white people. I have hated whites since I was a little girl. I have known that as a Christian I should love white people, but I couldn't help myself. I hated whites and wanted to get revenge. Tonight I have begun to love whites by faith, and it really works."

The young man added, "It worked for me, too; now my

hatred for whites is gone. Thank you for telling us how to love by faith."

People of one race who have hated those of other races have discovered God's supernatural love for each other. Christian husbands and wives who were living in conflict have claimed God's love by faith, and miracles have resulted. Parent-child struggles have been resolved and generation gaps have been bridged through loving by faith. Disputes in working situations have been resolved. Enemies cease to be enemies when you love them by faith. God's love has a way of dissolving prejudice and breaking down barriers.

Love is the greatest power known to man. It changed the course of the first-century world, and God is using it to bring a great revolution in the twenty-first century. Nothing can overcome God's love.

In the first century there was a wedding of love and faith resulting in a great spiritual revolution throughout the known world. Then both were lost during the Dark Ages. The realization of Martin Luther and his colleagues that the "just shall live by faith" ushered in the Reformation and another mighty movement of God's Spirit. But there was little love. In fact, there was often great conflict.

Today, God is bringing back to our remembrance the biblical wedding of the two—faith and love. Through faith, that supernatural, divine love of God will reach out where nothing else can go to capture men and women for Christ. The love that results from that faith will captivate people everywhere so that, as we live and love by faith, we will spread God's love throughout the world. This love is contagious, attractive, and aggressive. It creates hunger for God. It is active—constantly looking for loving things to do, people to uplift, and lives to change.

Take the First Step

*A*gape love frequently expresses itself as a flow of compassion. Jesus said, "Rivers of living water shall flow from the inmost being of anyone who believes in me" (John 7:38 TLB). Compassion is one of these rivers. It is a gentle stream of tenderness and concern for another person's need. Such love compelled Jesus to feed the hungry, comfort the sorrowing, heal the sick, teach the multitude, and raise the dead.

Most of us at some time in our lives have experienced this flow of love toward someone.

Perhaps you felt it while washing dishes, working on the job, driving down the freeway, or sitting in a classroom. You couldn't explain it, but your impulse was to do something special for that person.

I encourage you to take the first step; start loving by faith and follow that flow.

I encourage you to take the first step; start loving by faith and follow that flow. It is God's compassion streaming toward the one in need. The tug of love within you means that He is filling you with godly compassion and that He has chosen you to minister to that individual.

Ask God to manifest His tender compassion through you in some way today. As you pray, ask Him to lay someone on your heart. When you sense God's love flowing through you to that individual, find out his need and begin ministering to that need. By following the leading of God's Spirit, you can help those whom the Lord has prepared for His transforming touch, and you will become part of His miraculous provision. When God leads you to help someone, He will enable you to do what He leads you to do (Philippians 4:13; 1 Thessalonians 5:24).

A Japanese magazine has a picture of a butterfly on one of its pages. Its color is a dull gray until warmed by one's hand. The touch of a hand causes the special inks in the printing to react, and the dull gray is transformed into a flashing rainbow of color.

> *If Christ is in you, you are complete because Christ Himself is perfect love, perfect peace, perfect patience, perfect kindness.*

What other things can be thus changed by the warmth of your interest and *agape* love? Your family? Your church? Your city? This hurting world is hungry for the touch of someone who cares—who really cares! Through God's *agape* kind of love, you can be that someone.

WHO DON'T YOU LIKE?

But what about those who seem unlikable? People with whom you may have difficulty getting along? Individuals whose attitudes rub you the wrong way? I encourage you to make a list of people you do not like and begin to love them by faith.

HOW ABOUT YOURSELF?

Perhaps you will place yourself on the list. Have you thought of applying the truths of 1 Corinthians 13 to yourself by faith? Ask God to help you see yourself as He sees you. You have no reason to dislike yourself when your Creator has already for-given you and demonstrated His unconditional love by dying for you!

If Christ is in you, you are complete because Christ Himself is perfect love, perfect peace, perfect patience, per-fect kindness. He is all goodness, and He is in you!

Whenever Satan tries to attack you by reminding you of sins that you have already confessed or by magnifying your weaknesses and shortcomings, claim in faith the forgive-ness and righteousness of God, and thank Him that, on the authority of His Word, you do not have to be intimidated by Satan's accusation. Thank God that you are His child and that your sins are forgiven. Thank God that Satan has no control over you except that which is allowed by God. Then cast this care on the Lord as we are commanded to do in 1 Peter 5:7.

HOW ABOUT OTHERS?

Perhaps your boss, a fellow employee, your spouse, your children, or your father or mother is on the list of those whom you will love by faith. Pray for each person. Ask the Holy Spirit to fill you with Christ's love for all of them. Then, seek to meet with them as you draw upon God's lim-itless, inexhaustible, overwhelming love for them by faith. Expect God to work through you! Watch Him use your smile, your words, your patience to express His love for each individual.

Love by faith every one of your "enemies"—everyone who angers you, ignores you, bores you, or frustrates you. People are waiting to be loved with God's love.

A homemaker who, through a long, cold winter, had seen

her family through mumps, measles, a broken nose, three new teeth for the baby, and countless other difficulties, reached the point where these pressures and demands became too much for her. Finally, on her knees, she began to protest, "O Lord! I have so much to do!" But imagine her surprise when she heard herself say, "O Lord! I have so much to love!" You will never run out of opportunities to love by faith.

"The Fruit of the Spirit Is Love"

Remember, the *agape* kind of love is an act of the will, not just an emotion. You love *by faith*. By faith, you can claim God's love step by step, person by person.

"The fruit of the Spirit is love." Like fruit, love grows. Producing fruit requires a seed, then a flower, then pollination, then warm sun and refreshing rains, and even some contrary winds. Similarly in daily life, your love will be warmed by joy, watered by tears, and spread by the winds of circumstances. God uses all that you experience to work His will in your life. He is the One who makes your love grow. It is a continual, ever-increasing process. As Paul says, "May the Lord make your love to grow and overflow to each other and to everyone else" (1 Thessalonians 3:12 TLB).

How exciting it is to have such a dynamic, joyful force available to us! And it all comes from our loving Savior, Jesus Christ, who explicitly promises in His Word all that you need. You need not guess, or hope, or wish. You can claim this love by faith, right now, on the basis of God's command to love and His promise to answer whenever you pray for anything according to His will.

Why not make this prayer your own:

Lord, You would never have commanded me to love if You had not intended to enable me to do so. Therefore, right now, on the authority of Your command for me to love and on the authority of Your promise to answer if I ask anything according to Your will, I personally claim Your love—the 1 Corinthians 13 kind of love—for You, for all people, and for myself. Amen.

Appendix B

God's Word on Total Forgiveness

Following are selected Scripture references that were presented throughout the text of this book. We encourage you to sit down with your Bible and review these verses in their context, prayerfully reflecting upon what God's Word tells you about the joy of total forgiveness.

CHAPTER 1

Psalm 103:12

Luke 5:18–24

CHAPTER 2

Psalm 103:11–12

Hebrews 10:10, 14, 18

John 3:16–17

Romans 8:1–2

Romans 3:23

John 15:13

Colossians 1:21–22

Colossians 2:13–14

1 Corinthians 6:11

John 8:36

John 8:11

CHAPTER 3

Psalm 32:6

Acts 13:22

Psalm 51:1–4

Psalm 32:1–5

Hebrews 12:6

John 17:22–23

Luke 15:11–32

Hebrews 12:1

Revelation 2:4

1 Corinthians 6:19

CHAPTER 4

Psalm 66:18

CHAPTER 5

1 John 1:9

1 John 1:6–7

Proverbs 14:9

1 John 1:8, 10

CHAPTER 6

Psalm 139:23–24
Psalm 103:12
Micah 7:19
Hebrews 8:12;
  10:17

CHAPTER 7

Hebrews 10:16–19

John 10:10
1 John 4:18–19
1 John 3:14–16
Matthew 18:21–35
Acts 1:8

CHAPTER 8

Isaiah 40:29–31
Galatians 5:5

Galatians 5:22–23
Romans 8:29

CHAPTER 9

John 15:4–5
Hebrews 13:5
Philippians 1:21

About the Author

DR. BILL BRIGHT, fueled by his passion to share the love and claims of Jesus Christ with "every living person on earth," was the founder and president of Campus Crusade for Christ. The world's largest Christian ministry, Campus Crusade serves people in 191 countries through a staff of 26,000 full-time employees and more than 225,000 trained volunteers working in some sixty targeted ministries and projects that range from military ministry to inner-city ministry.

Bill Bright was so motivated by what is known as the Great Commission, Christ's command to carry the gospel throughout the world, that in 1956 he wrote a booklet titled *The Four Spiritual Laws*, which has been printed in 200 languages and distributed to more than 2.5 billion people. Other books Bright authored include *Discover the Book God Wrote, God: Discover His Character, Come Help Change Our World, The Holy Spirit: The Key to Supernatural Living, Life Without Equal, Witnessing Without Fear, Coming Revival, Journey Home,* and *Red Sky in the Morning.*

In 1979 Bright commissioned the *JESUS* film, a feature-length dramatization of the life of Christ. To date, the film has been viewed by more than 5.7 billion people in 191 countries and has become the most widely viewed and translated film in history.

Dr. Bright died in July 2003 before the final editing of this book. But he prayed that it would leave a legacy of his love for Jesus and the power of the Holy Spirit to change lives. He is survived by his wife, Vonette; their sons and daughters-in-law; and four grandchildren.

THE LIFETIME TEACHINGS OF

Written by one of Christianity's most respected and beloved teachers, this series is a must for every believer's library. Each of the books in the series focuses on a vital aspect of a meaningful life of faith: trusting God, accepting Christ, living a spirit-filled life, intimacy with God, forgiveness, prayer, obedience, supernatural thinking, giving, and sharing Christ with others.

Dr. Bill Bright was the founder of Campus Crusade for Christ Intl., the world's largest Christian ministry. He commissioned the JESUS film, a documentary on the life of Christ that has been translated into more than 800 languages.

EACH BOOK INCLUDES A CELEBRITY-READ ABRIDGED AUDIO CD!

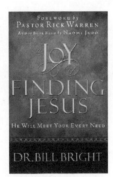

Joy of Trusting God
Foreword by Billy Graham
Audio by John Tesh
0-78144-246-X

Joy of Finding Jesus
Foreword by Pastor
Rick Warren
Audio by Naomi Judd
0-78144-247-8

Joy of Spirit-Filled Living
Foreword by Kay Arthur
Audio by Ricky Skaggs
0-78144-248-6

DR. BILL BRIGHT

FOUNDER OF CAMPUS CRUSADE FOR CHRIST

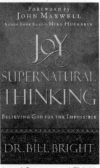

Joy of Supernatural Thinking
Foreword by John Maxwell
Audio by Gov. Mike Huckabee
0-78144-253-2

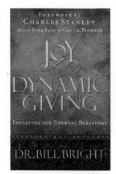

Joy of Dynamic Giving
Foreword by Charles Stanley
Audio by John Schneider
0-78144-254-0

Joy of Sharing Jesus
Foreword by Pat Robertson
Audio by Kathie Lee Gifford
0-78144-255-9

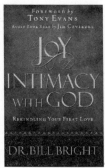

Joy of Intimacy with God
Foreword by Tony Evans
Audio by Amy Grant
0-78144-249-4

Joy of Total Forgiveness
Foreword by Gary Smalley
Audio by Janine Turner
0-78144-250-8

Joy of Active Prayer
Foreword by Max Lucado
Audio by Joni Earekcson Tada
0-78144-251-6

Joy of Faithful Obedience
Foreword by Tim LaHaye
Audio by Kirk Franklin
0-78144-252-4

Collect all 10 of These Foundational Works!

Additional copies of
THE JOY OF TOTAL FORGIVENESS
and other titles in "The Joy of Knowing God" series
are available wherever good books are sold.

✝ ✝ ✝

If you have enjoyed this book,
or if it has had an impact on your life,
we would like to hear from you.

Please contact us at:

VICTOR BOOKS
Cook Communications Ministries, Dept. 201
4050 Lee Vance View
Colorado Springs, CO 80918

Or at our Web site: www.cookministries.com

Victor®
The Bible Teacher's Teacher

The Word at Work Around the World

A vital part of Cook Communications Ministries is our international outreach, Cook Communications Ministries International (CCMI). Your purchase of this book, and of other books and Christian-growth products from Cook, enables CCMI to provide Bibles and Christian literature to people in more than 150 languages in 65 countries.

Cook Communications Ministries is a not-for-profit, self-supporting organization. Revenues from sales of our books, Bible curricula, and other church and home products not only fund our U.S. ministry, but also fund our CCMI ministry around the world. One hundred percent of donations to CCMI go to our international literature programs.

CCMI reaches out internationally in three ways:

· Our premier International Christian Publishing Institute (ICPI) trains leaders from nationally led publishing houses around the world.

· We provide literature for pastors, evangelists, and Christian workers in their national language.

· We reach people at risk—refugees, AIDS victims, street children, and famine victims—with God's Word.

Word Power, God's Power

Faith Kidz, RiverOak, Honor, Life Journey, Victor, NexGen — every time you purchase a book produced by Cook Communications Ministries, you not only meet a vital personal need in your life or in the life of someone you love, but you're also a part of ministering to José in Colombia, Humberto in Chile, Gousa in India, or Lidiane in Brazil. You help make it possible for a pastor in China, a child in Peru, or a mother in West Africa to enjoy a life-changing book. And because you helped, children and adults around the world are learning God's Word and walking in his ways.

Thank you for your partnership in helping to disciple the world. May God bless you with the power of his Word in your life.

For more information about our international ministries, visit www.ccmi.org.